The World At Our Table

A fresh approach to cooking from down home and around the world.

Woodward Academy Parents Club
Atlanta, Georgia

For additional copies of *The World At Our Table,* use the order form in the back of this book or send a check for $17.95 plus $3.50 shipping and handling (Georgia residents, add 6% sales tax per book) to:

*The World
At Our Table*
Woodward Academy
Parents Club
1662 Rugby Avenue
College Park,
Georgia 30337
404-765-8200

Printed in the USA by

WIMMER

The Wimmer Companies, Inc.
Memphis

Woodward Academy seeks to provide a well-rounded college preparatory education in a structured and caring environment. On its three campuses throughout the metro-Atlanta area, strong programs have been developed in all areas of academics, within the performing and visual arts, and in athletics. Since 1900, the Academy has sought to prepare each student for his own tomorrow. In the words of Academy founder John Charles Woodward, "It is the aim of the Academy to find the needs, as well as the aptitudes, of every pupil...to enable him to find his best and largest self."

The motto, "Every Opportunity for Every Student," expresses Woodward's commitment to making a positive difference in each student's education.

ABOUT OUR ARTIST

Former Woodward parent, Mimi Shaw, whose art graces our cover and chapter pages, exhibits in some of the South's premier galleries, including the Ann Jacob Gallery (Atlanta, Georgia, and Highlands, North Carolina) and The Left Bank Art Gallery (St. Simon's Island, Georgia). Her work is owned by corporate and private collectors throughout the United States and Europe.

*special thanks
for graphic design assistance
to **Newsletters Plus**, Atlanta, GA
for planning and production help
to the Woodward Academy Development Staff*

Introduction

As Atlanta has grown into an international city, Atlantans have remained steeped in the best Southern traditions — hospitality, generosity and a hearty appreciation of good home cooking.

Woodward Academy has grown along with Atlanta. When planning this cookbook, we hoped the recipes we gathered would reflect the richly varied heritage that makes our school community unique. But we never dreamed just what a tremendous buffet of flavors we would be able to offer. On the following pages you will find not only time-honored Southern classics and New South innovations, but a host of family favorites reflecting our students' many culinary and cultural roots around the globe.

Chock full of regional flavors and fresh ingredients, *The World At Our Table* is also a book designed for today's practical, health-conscious cooks. Our recipes offer time-saving tips, storage advice and serving suggestions.

The world is indeed at our table. Pull up a chair, take a plate (and a mixing spoon) and join in.

Cookbook Committee 1994-1996

CO-CHAIRMEN
D.D. Cardwell   Beverly Burdette

CHAIRMAN ELECT
Charlotte Schroeder

EDITOR
Liza Nelson Brown

MARKETING COORDINATOR
Carol Curran

PROJECT MANAGER
Elizabeth Marshall Tilden

BUSINESS MANAGER
Liz Thorneloe

TESTING COORDINATOR
Jan Perkins

PARENTS CLUB
Joan Ansley

COMPUTER COORDINATOR
Pat King

DEVELOPMENT ADVISOR
Holly Wilbourn

TREASURERS
Carol Hastey   Marty Wilson

VOLUNTEER COORDINATORS
June Miller   Sharon Stewart

HOSPITALITY
Coordinator: Esther Garges
Ann Warsham   Alicia Mitchell

CORRESPONDING SECRETARY
Nancy Barksdale

SECTION COORDINATORS
Lynne Anservitz   Arlene Crump   Susan Fuller   Judy Gallagher
Mary Ellen Gilmore   Sue Griffin   Cheryl Henard   Alicia Mitchell
Kathleen Saurer   Polly Stevenson   Cappa Woodward   Jamie Wyatt

MARKETING COMMITTEE
Assistant Coordinator: Vickie Garrett
Nancy Lassiter   Cleo Hudson   Carol McElheney, Georgia Watts
Lisa Calkins, Lynne Anservitz   Betsy Cathell, Henrietta Kisseih
Jan Perkins, Susan Fuller   Cathy Hubbard, Janis Meyrowitz

SCHOOL EVENTS COMMITTEE
Coordinator: Scotty Pannell
Dianne Walker   Dora Parramore   Peggy Bosse   Linda Elliott
Lisa Long, Sherry Burks   Andrea Booth, Penny Anne Machemehl

Table of Contents

The shadow of a magnolia blossom graces those recipes
we consider traditional Southern classics.

*We dedicate this book
to the memory of Janet McEnerny
whose enthusiasm, courage and generosity of spirit
inspired us all.*

Appetizers
and
Savory Snacks

Appetizers and Savory Snacks

HOT APPETIZERS

LITTLE PIZZAS

COLD APPETIZERS

Menu
Cocktails on the Veranda..........11

SANDWICHES

SPREADS, PATÉS, DIPS

SAUCES

SPECIAL EXTRAS

Blue Cheese Figs With Prosciutto

18 figs, fresh or dried
½ cup crumbled blue cheese
6 paper-thin slices prosciutto

Slice figs almost, but not completely, down middle. With finger, press indentation in soft insides of figs. Spoon about 1 teaspoon cheese into each fig and press fig closed around it. Wrap each fig with ⅓ slice prosciutto. Can do ahead to this point and keep, refrigerated, up to 4 hours until ready to serve.

Place figs on ungreased cookie sheet and run under broiler to melt cheese, less than 1 minute. Do NOT microwave.

Makes 18 figs

*quick and easy
can do ahead*

Variations:

These are also good using dates instead of figs, or try serving some of each. You might also consider adding 1 tablespoon chopped walnuts to the blue cheese filling.

Feta and Scallion Stuffed Mushroom Caps

1 pound medium mushrooms, stems removed
5 tablespoons melted butter, or as needed
¼ cup lemon juice, approximately
8 ounces mashed feta cheese
½ cup cream cheese, room temperature
½ cup grated Parmesan cheese
½ cup minced scallions or
  green onions, some green included
¼ cup minced parsley
1 egg
½ cup crumbled garlic croutons

Preheat oven to 350°.

Clean mushroom caps. Combine melted butter and lemon juice. Brush onto caps inside and out.

Combine cheeses, scallions, parsley, egg and croutons. Mound high on mushroom caps.

Place on lightly greased cookie sheet and bake until piping hot, 10-12 minutes, then broil a few seconds to brown.

Serves 6-10

*quick and easy
can do ahead*

Mushroom Croustades

12 slices white bread
    butter to spread
    oil for sautéing

8   ounces chopped mushrooms
3   tablespoons chopped sweet onion
3   tablespoons chopped sweet red or green pepper
2   tablespoons flour
1   cup evaporated milk
1   teaspoon salt
½   teaspoon lemon juice
1   tablespoon parsley
½   teaspoon cayenne pepper
    Parmesan or Romano cheese

Preheat oven to 400°.

To make croustades, cut bread into rounds with cookie cutter, then butter. Butter muffin tin and place a bread round in each muffin cup, forming shell. Bake at 400° until lightly browned, about 10 minutes.

Sauté mushrooms, onions and peppers in small amount of oil. Add flour and milk. Cook until thickened and add seasonings. Cook a few more minutes, until ingredients are well incorporated.

Fill croustades with mixture and top with Parmesan cheese. Bake in 400° oven until cheese melts and croustades are heated through, about 8 minutes.

Serves 12

 can freeze

Hot Cheese Puffs

1 loaf French bread
8 ounces cheddar or Monterey Jack cheese with jalapeños
⅓ cup margarine
3 ounces cream cheese
2 egg whites, room temperature

Cube French bread into 1-inch cubes.

Melt cheese, margarine and cream cheese over low heat, preferably in double boiler.

Beat egg whites until stiff. Fold into cheese mixture. Keep cheese mixture warm.

Dip bread cubes into warm cheese mixture.

Place on cookie sheets and freeze. When frozen, place cubes in plastic bags and store until needed, up to 3 months.

Preheat oven to 400° and bake 10 minutes before serving.

Makes 5-6 dozen puffs

easy
do ahead

Menu

Cocktails on the Veranda

Summer Marinated Shrimp
24

Bourbon Mushrooms
168

Country Pâté Madeira
33

Hot Cheese Puffs
11

Crudités with Lemon Garlic Bean Dip
37

Toasted Pita Triangles
36

Czechoslovakians
213

Double Chocolate Brownies
224

Variations:

In addition to the vegetables traditionally used, you might try bell pepper strips, carrot sticks, sweet potatoes and broccoli flowerets.

Cook's Tip:

"Mise en place" is a French culinary term that refers to having all ingredients prepped and all equipment necessary for a given recipe at hand before beginning to cook. When everything you need is set out in front of you, cooking is a more enjoyable enterprise, and you'll be less likely to forget that crucial ingredient.

Vegetable Pakoris

In India, these fritters are usually eaten with tea, but given their spicy, slightly salty flavor, they are also perfect as a cocktail hors d'oeuvre.

¾ cup water
1 cup sifted chickpea flour*
¼ teaspoon salt
¼ teaspoon ground cumin
¼ teaspoon turmeric
¼ teaspoon baking soda
⅛ teaspoon freshly ground black pepper, or to taste
⅛ teaspoon cayenne pepper, or to taste

1 medium potato, peeled and cut into ¹⁄₁₆-inch slices (keep in bowl of cold water until ready to use)
1 small head cauliflower broken into 1-inch flowerets
1 medium onion, cut into ¹⁄₁₆-inch thick rings
oil for deep frying
salt and pepper for sprinkling over cooked pakoris

Gradually mix ¾ cup water with chickpea flour to make batter thick enough to coat vegetables. Add remaining batter ingredients and mix well.

Heat oil in skillet over low flame until hot but not smoking. Dip a few vegetables in batter (be sure to wipe potato slices dry first) and drop into oil. Cook 4-5 minutes on each side, until vegetables cook through and turn golden brown. Remove with slotted spoon and drain on paper towels. Sprinkle with salt and pepper while hot. Continue with rest of vegetables.

Pakoris are best served while crisp and hot. Purchased chutney can be used as dip.

Serves 6-8

*Chickpea flour can be purchased in Indian grocery stores, gourmet food shops or gourmet sections of supermarkets.

Sambousiks

Though these curried pasties take a little work, they are definite crowd pleasers.

1	tablespoon butter
1	tablespoon flour
½	teaspoon salt
¾	cup scalded milk
1	teaspoon curry powder
2	teaspoons lime juice
1	medium onion, chopped
1	green chili, chopped
1	garlic clove, minced
¼	teaspoon ground ginger
¼	teaspoon turmeric
¼	teaspoon coriander
¼	teaspoon chili powder
¼	teaspoon celery seed
½	teaspoon cumin
⅛	teaspoon allspice
1½	cups minced cooked chicken, beef or lamb
1¼	cups sifted all-purpose flour
1	teaspoon salt
¾	tablespoon butter
3-4	tablespoons ice water
¼	cup egg white wash

Melt 1 tablespoon butter in saucepan. Blend in 1 tablespoon flour and ½ teaspoon salt. Gradually add milk, stirring to boiling point. Add lime juice, onion, chili and seasonings. Cook over low heat 5 minutes. Add meat and mix lightly. Adjust seasonings. Filling may be made 1-2 days ahead and refrigerated.

Sift flour with ½ teaspoon salt. With pastry blender, cut in butter. Gradually add ice water, tossing lightly until dough forms a ball. Chill 15 minutes, then roll out on lightly floured board. Fold dough in half, then quarters. Roll out again and fold into thirds. Wrap in wax paper and chill 1 hour.

Preheat oven to 375°.

Roll out dough ⅛-inch thick on lightly floured board and cut into 3-inch circles with cookie or biscuit cutter. Place scant tablespoon of meat mixture in center, fold over dough and seal edges with fork. Brush with egg white wash. Prick top. Bake at 375° until golden brown, about 15 minutes. Serve hot or at room temperature.

Makes 24

can do ahead

Cook's Tip:

Box pie crust mix or refrigerator ready pie crust works in place of homemade dough in this recipe. The box crust will be flakier and more tender while the ready made crust will have a prettier baked finish.

Cook's Tip:

To make an egg white wash, mix an egg white with enough water to equal ¼ cup. For a more golden pastry, brush with 1 whole beaten egg.

Cook's Tip:

*Technically, scallions
are the shoots of
white onions only;
green onion shoots
may be substituted if
scallions are
unavailable.*

Spanakopita

The classic Greek spinach and cheese pie

	olive oil
2	bunches scallions, minced
3	8-ounce boxes frozen chopped spinach, defrosted and pressed dry
½	cup minced fresh parsley
½	teaspoon dried dill weed
8	eggs, beaten
1	pound crumbled feta cheese
¼	teaspoon nutmeg
	salt
1	1-pound box phyllo dough
	non stick vegetable oil spray (olive or canola)

Preheat oven to 350°.

Sauté scallions in a little olive oil until tender. Set aside. Combine spinach, parsley, dill, beaten eggs, cheese and nutmeg. Add cooked scallions. Season lightly with salt and mix well.

Grease 9x13-inch glass baking dish. Line with five sheets of phyllo, spraying each sheet with vegetable oil spray. Spread spinach mixture over phyllo and top with remaining sheets of phyllo, again spraying with oil between layers. Spray top sheet. Refrigerate until ready to proceed, up to 24 hours.

Bake in 350° oven 45 minutes.

Let rest for a few minutes, then cut into squares and serve hot or cold.

Serves 10-15

 can do ahead

Sesame Chicken Fingers

- 6 boneless chicken breast halves or
  2 pounds packaged chicken finger strips
- 1½ cups buttermilk
- 2 tablespoons lemon juice
- 2 teaspoons Worcestershire sauce
- 1 teaspoon soy sauce
- 1 teaspoon paprika
- 1 tablespoon Greek seasoning,
  available in most supermarkets
- 1 teaspoon salt
- 1 teaspoon pepper
- 2 garlic cloves, minced

- 4 cups soft breadcrumbs
- ½ cup sesame seeds
- ¼ cup melted butter
- ¼ cup melted shortening

Cut chicken into ½-inch strips. Combine next 9 ingredients, add chicken and mix until well coated. Cover and refrigerate overnight. Preheat oven to 350°.

Drain chicken thoroughly. Combine bread crumbs and sesame seeds until well mixed. Add chicken and toss to coat. Place chicken in 2 greased 13x9x2-inch baking pans. Combine melted butter and shortening. Drizzle over chicken. Bake at 350° for 35-40 minutes. Serve hot with warm plum sauce or honey mustard.

Makes about 24 portions

 marinating overnight required

Plum Sauce

- 1½ cups red plum jam
- 1½ tablespoons prepared mustard
- 1½ tablespoons prepared horseradish
- 1½ teaspoons lemon juice

Combine ingredients in small sauce pan. Heat over low heat, stirring constantly until warm.

Little Pizzas

Who does not love pizza? Whether you use store bought crust or make your own, pizza is easy to prepare and impressive to serve. Here is a varied sampling of possible topping combinations. Try one at a time or mix and match.

Unless otherwise noted, all these pizzas should be baked in a pre-heated 450° oven for approximately 10 minutes, or until the bottom of the crust is brown. Use a pizza stone or well greased pizza pan for baking. Ingredient amounts depend on the size of your crust.

Thai Chicken Pizza

- 1-2 teaspoons hot chili or garlic oil
- ¼ cup grated fontina cheese
- ⅓ cup grated mozzarella cheese
- 1 chicken breast half, grilled and cut into chunks
- 1-2 tablespoons Thai peanut sauce, available in most large groceries
- ¼ cup grated carrot
- ¼ cup chopped green onion

- ¼ cup chopped dry roasted peanuts
- ¼ cup bean sprouts
- 2 tablespoons chopped cilantro

Brush crust lightly with oil. Top with cheeses, then chicken chunks that have been tossed in Thai peanut sauce. Add grated carrot and chopped green onion. Bake at 450° for 8-10 minutes.

After baking, remove from oven and scatter chopped cilantro, peanuts, and bean sprouts over pizza.

Makes 1 10-inch pizza

Pizza Crust

Store-bought pizza crusts work fine, but if you're a pizza purist, you will want to make your own. Consider making a number of crusts at one time, then freezing for future use.

- 2¾ cups warm water
- 1 package dry yeast (a scant tablespoon)
- 6½ cups bread flour
- 1 tablespoon salt

Dissolve yeast in warm water (about 10 minutes).

Combine 6 cups flour with salt in large bowl. Gradually add water and yeast. Stir until soft, shaggy dough forms. Cover bowl and allow to rest 10 minutes.

Turn out onto well-floured surface and knead, adding flour as needed, until smooth and elastic. Keep hands well floured but avoid adding too much extra flour. Dough should be soft, not dry. Place in large, well-oiled bowl and turn dough in oil to coat.

continued on next page

Sundried Tomato and Goat Cheese Pizza

1 teaspoon garlic oil, or more as needed
¼ cup sliced sundried tomatoes packed in oil
3 tablespoons goat cheese
2 tablespoons chopped fresh basil leaves

Place sundried tomatoes with garlic oil in food processor or blender and blend until smooth paste forms.

Spread tomato paste over crusts and crumble goat cheese on top. Sprinkle with chopped basil leaves. Bake in 450° oven 8 minutes.

Makes 1 7-inch pizza

Black Bean and Sundried Tomato Pizza

1 teaspoon garlic oil, or more as needed
⅓ cup grated cheddar cheese
⅓ cup grated Monterey Jack cheese
⅓ cup black beans, drained
⅛ teaspoon each of ground coriander, cumin, chili powder and garlic powder
4 sundried tomatoes, packed in oil, sliced
¼ cup julienne sliced dried chorizo sausage
   chopped fresh cilantro to taste, optional

Brush pizza crust with oil and sprinkle with cheddar and Monterey Jack cheeses. Season black beans with spices and scatter seasoned beans over cheese along with thin slices of sundried tomato and julienne of dried chorizo. Do not completely cover crust with beans; you should be able to see cheese underneath. Bake at 450° for 10 minutes.

After baking, sprinkle with fresh chopped cilantro if desired.

Makes 1 10-inch pizza

continued from previous page
Cover bowl with plastic and allow to rise 3-4 hours. (Or place in large 2-gallon zip lock bag and refrigerate overnight or up to 24 hours. Return to room temperature.)

Punch down dough and divide into 3 pieces for large pizzas, or 6-8 pieces for individual pizzas. Cover and let rest 30 minutes. Roll out dough and top with topping of your choice.

To save for future use, place dough without topping on pizza stone or lightly greased pan and bake at 425° for 3-4 minutes or until dough firms up but is not brown. Cool and refrigerate or freeze. When ready to use, remove from freezer and let sit at room temperature about 20 minutes. Then proceed with topping.

Garlic Oil

Stir 1 clove crushed garlic into ½ cup good olive oil.

Allow to sit about 30 minutes before using, but be sure to refrigerate if kept longer. Once refrigerated, homemade garlic oil should be used within 3 days.

Gorgonzola and Walnut Pizza

1 teaspoon olive oil
3 tablespoons crumbled Gorgonzola cheese
¼ cup chopped walnuts
  freshly ground black pepper to taste

Brush crust lightly with oil. Sprinkle with Gorgonzola. Scatter chopped walnuts on top and add a grinding of fresh black pepper. Bake at 450° for 8-10 minutes.

This is wonderful served with sliced pears.

Makes 1 7-inch pizza

easy
do ahead

Cook's Tip:

Whenever you light your grill, throw a few vegetables on to cook and save for another meal. Good grilling candidates include onions, whole garlic heads, peppers, sliced eggplant and mushrooms. These will keep 3-4 days refrigerated.

Grilled Vegetable and Feta Pizza

2 tablespoons olive oil
5 mushrooms, thickly sliced
½ red pepper
½ green pepper
4 ⅓-inch slices eggplant
1-2 teaspoons chili or garlic oil
¼ cup feta cheese

Brush vegetables lightly with olive oil and grill until browned and tender. Chop or slice all vegetables.

Brush crust lightly with chili or garlic oil. Top with vegetables and scatter crumbled feta over vegetables. Bake at 450° for 8-10 minutes.

Makes 1 10-inch pizza

easy
do ahead

Arugula Pesto and Parmesan Pizza

½ cup arugula pesto
3 tablespoons Parmesan cheese

Spread pesto thinly over crust and sprinkle with Parmesan cheese. Bake at 450° for 8-10 minutes.

Makes 1 10-inch pizza

Arugula Pesto

2 cups packed arugula, stems removed
4 garlic cloves, peeled
¼ cup pistachio nuts
⅓ cup extra virgin olive oil
½ cup freshly grated Parmesan cheese
salt and pepper to taste

Place arugula, garlic and nuts in food processor with steel blade. Process until finely chopped. With machine running, add half the oil in a slow stream. Turn processor off and add cheese. Process until smooth, then add remaining oil. Season to taste.

 *easy
do ahead*

Onion, Prosciutto and Parmesan Pizzette

⅔ cup caramelized onions
1 ounce very thinly sliced prosciutto
2 tablespoons freshly grated Parmesan cheese or to taste

Spread onion mixture over crust. Top with prosciutto and sprinkle with Parmesan. Bake at 450° for 8-10 minutes.

Makes 1 7-inch pizza

 *easy
do ahead*

Caramelized Onions

3 large onions, preferably Vidalia
¼ cup olive oil
salt to taste

Thinly slice onions and place in skillet with heated oil over low heat. Let onions cook at least one hour. Stir occasionally. Onions should be caramel color. These are good on sandwiches and mixed into pasta as well as on pizza.

California Quesadillas

Variations:

You can eliminate olives and add diced, cooked chicken, chopped spinach, cooked chopped shrimp or cooked potato cubes.

2½ cups shredded Monterey Jack cheese
1 6-ounce jar marinated artichoke hearts, drained and chopped
⅓ cup pitted and chopped kalamata olives
⅔ cup jalapeño salsa (page 26)
½ cup toasted slivered almonds
¼ cup loosely packed chopped fresh cilantro
12 flour tortillas
3 tablespoons butter

Preheat oven to 450°.

Combine cheese, artichokes, olives, salsa, almonds and cilantro in large bowl and mix well.

Brush 1 side of 1 tortilla with butter and place buttered side down on baking sheet. Place ⅙ of cheese mixture on tortillas, spreading to within ¾-inch of the edge. Top with second tortilla, press firmly and brush top lightly with butter. Repeat with remaining tortillas.

Bake each quesadilla approximately 10 minutes or until lightly browned. Let stand 5 minutes to cool before cutting.

Serve with jalapeño salsa.

Serves 8-10

 easy

Antipasto

1 pound thinly sliced Genoa salami

¾ pound mozzarella cheese,
cut into ¼-inch thick rectangular slices

1 large can chickpeas, drained

1 large jar marinated artichoke hearts, cubed

4 red peppers, roasted and cut in long, thin strips or
from jar

1-2 cups Greek or kalamata olives

On large, round serving platter, layer salami in overlapping circular pattern to center. Place mounded chick peas on top of salami in center of platter. Place olives in circular pattern around chickpeas. From olives, begin alternating pattern of roasted pepper strips, mozzarella slices and cubed artichoke hearts. Pattern should lie so it appears pointing from edge of platter toward chick peas. Can prepare several hours before serving.

Serve with crusty baguette.

Serves 6-8

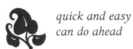 *quick and easy
can do ahead*

Bruschetta

Variations:

The topping is good on untoasted French bread. This combination of ingredients also works as a sauce. Add to hot spaghetti with a little Parmesan cheese grated over it.

4   medium ripe Roma tomatoes, diced
1   tablespoon diced red onion
2   tablespoons diced red bell pepper
2   garlic cloves, pressed

8   large fresh basil leaves
2   tablespoons extra virgin olive oil

1   small sourdough or French baguette
½   cup freshly grated Parmesan
    salt and freshly ground pepper

Combine first 4 ingredients in bowl.

Bunch basil leaves together tightly. Slice thin with a sharp knife or scissors into long, thin strips. Add to mixture.

Add olive oil to combined ingredients. Season with salt and pepper. Cover and set aside for at least 1 hour. It is best used the day it is made.

Slice bread diagonally to form long thin slices. Toast or grill until both sides are golden. Spoon mixture over toasted bread. Top with freshly grated Parmesan cheese and freshly ground pepper. Serve at room temperature.

Serves 4

 easy

Shrimp Remoulade

Take your pick: the version with anchovies or the version without.

Anchovy Remoulade
- 2 tablespoons minced fresh parsley
- 2 teaspoons minced fresh tarragon or 1 teaspoon dried
- 2 teaspoons minced sweet pickle
- 1 tablespoon minced capers
- 1 garlic clove, minced
- ½ teaspoon anchovy paste or 2 flat anchovies, minced
- 1 tablespoon paprika or Cajun seasoning
- 1 medium fresh red bell pepper, seeded and coarsely chopped
- ½ cup mayonnaise
- ¼ cup Dijon mustard
- 1 tablespoon freshly squeezed lemon juice
- 1 tablespoon prepared horseradish salt and pepper to taste
- 1 pound large shrimp, boiled, shelled with tails attached and deveined

In food processor or blender, puree parsley, tarragon, pickles, capers, garlic, anchovies, bell pepper and paprika or Cajun seasoning. Place in small bowl. Blend in mayonnaise, lemon juice, mustard and horseradish. Season to taste with salt and pepper.

Refrigerate sauce 2 hours or up to 2 days before serving with shrimp.

Red Remoulade
- 1 red bell pepper, roasted and peeled (page 21)
- 1 cup mayonnaise
- 1 scallion, minced
- 1 lemon's worth of zest, minced (tip, page 25)
- ¼ cup minced dill pickle
- 2 tablespoons freshly grated horseradish, or prepared
- 1 tablespoon capers
- ¼ cup chopped fresh parsley
- 1 pound large shrimp, boiled, shelled with tails attached and deveined

Puree pepper with mayonnaise in food processor or blender. Add remaining ingredients except shrimp and puree until almost smooth. Chill at least 30 minutes before serving with boiled shrimp.

Serves 4-6

easy
do ahead

Variations:

Remoulade sauce is delicous over crab claws, crab cakes, scallops, shrimp or grilled fish. You can use it as a dipping sauce, or consider marinating shrimp, tails up, in the sauce, then letting guests pick out shrimp from the remoulade by their tails.

Summer Marinated Shrimp

Use a glass bowl if possible because the mix of colors is very inviting.

3 pounds large fresh shrimp, cooked and deveined
2 sweet Vidalia onions, sliced
3 fresh tomatoes, peeled and sliced
2 large fresh lemons, sliced thin

1 cup olive oil
¼ cup red wine vinegar
2 cloves garlic, minced
1 teaspoon Worcestershire sauce
2 teaspoons sugar
½ teaspoon black pepper
½ teaspoon celery salt

In a large shallow bowl, preferably glass, layer shrimp, tomatoes, onions and lemons.

Mix remaining ingredients and pour over shrimp mixture.

Chill several hours before serving.

Serve with crackers and toothpicks.

Serves 50

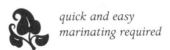

*quick and easy
marinating required*

Stuffed Belgian Endive

5	small heads of Belgian endive
1	pound very fresh uncooked salmon fillet
¼	cup fresh lemon juice
2	teaspoons mayonnaise
2	tablespoons grainy mustard
2	tablespoons finely chopped parsley
¼	teaspoon white pepper
1	tablespoon rinsed and drained capers
1	tablespoon hot red pepper sauce

Carefully separate leaves of endive, rinse, pat dry and chill.

Coarsely chop salmon in food processor, remove to bowl and add all ingredients except capers and hot sauce. Blend well. Gently stir in capers. Season with hot sauce. Stuff individual endive leaves, cover with plastic wrap and refrigerate 2 hours.

Serves 12

 quick and easy
should do ahead

Sparta Cheese Straws

1½	cups butter
1¼	pounds New York state sharp-cheddar cheese, grated (about 5 cups)
½	teaspoon prepared horseradish
4	cups sifted all-purpose flour
½	teaspoon garlic salt
½	teaspoon cayenne pepper
½	teaspoon onion salt

Preheat oven to 300°.

Cream butter, cheese and horseradish together well. Sift remaining ingredients together. Add to cheese mixture. Thoroughly mix with fingers. Run through cookie press or chill, roll out on floured board and cut into desired shapes. Bake in 300° oven for 25-30 minutes.

Remove from pan and cool before serving or storing in air-tight container.

Makes over 150 straws

 *can do ahead*
can freeze

Cook's Tip:

Before squeezing fresh lemon for juice, carefully remove lemon peel with lemon zester or sharp paring knife. Place zest in sealed plastic bag and keep frozen for future use.

Variations:

Instead of raw salmon, try smoked salmon. You can also stuff endive with a mixture of cream cheese and julienned ham slices.

Jalapeño Salsa

This is so tasty and easy to make, you may never buy the bottled stuff again.

1   large garlic clove, minced
2   (or more) medium fresh jalapeños, minced
5   radishes, minced
1   bunch green onions (about 6)
½   green bell pepper, chopped
1   tablespoon grated onion
2   28-ounce cans peeled plum tomatoes, chopped with juice
¾   cup chopped fresh cilantro

Mix all ingredients. Best made 1 day ahead. Serve with chips, tacos or any recipe that calls for salsa.

Tortilla Roll Ups

8   ounces cream cheese, low or no-fat okay
1   tablespoon grated onion
1   tablespoon plus 2 teaspoons jalapeño salsa
1½   teaspoons ground cumin

4   9-inch flour tortillas
⅓   cup finely chopped green pepper
⅓   cup finely chopped red pepper
3   tablespoons finely chopped green onion
3   tablespoons sliced or chopped black olives
¼   cup chopped fresh cilantro

Mix first 4 ingredients and spread evenly over tortillas. (If tortillas are fresh or from a freshly opened package, you may want them to sit at room temperature a few minutes to "dry out" a little. If too moist, they may get sticky when you roll and refrigerate.) Sprinkle red peppers, green peppers, chopped onion, black olives and cilantro over cheese spread. Roll up each tortilla jelly roll style.

Roll tortillas in waxed paper and place in plastic bag. Refrigerate several hours before cutting into 1-inch bite size pieces. You may serve on a tray with the rest of the salsa as dip.

Makes about 30 pieces

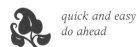

*quick and easy
do ahead*

Smoked Oyster Roll

8 ounces cream cheese, low or no-fat okay
1 tablespoon mayonnaise, low or no-fat okay
1 teaspoon white wine Worcestershire sauce
1 dash hot red pepper sauce
1 small garlic clove, minced
1 3¾-ounce can smoked oysters, drained
1 tablespoon lemon juice
1 bunch fresh parsley, chopped
2 teaspoons finely grated onion

Mix cream cheese, mayonnaise, Worcestershire sauce, hot red pepper sauce and garlic. Spread about ½-inch thick on waxed paper. Mash oysters with fork and spread on top of cheese mixture. Sprinkle with fresh lemon juice. Cover with waxed paper and chill until firm, at least 1 hour.

Remove waxed paper and roll like jelly roll. Wrap in plastic wrap and refrigerate at least 2 hours, preferably overnight.

Before serving, roll in chopped parsley combined with grated onion. Serve with plain crackers.

Serves 10

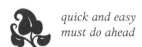
*quick and easy
must do ahead*

Sandwiches

The sandwich is a remarkable invention. Simple to prepare, and simple to eat, it offers limitless possibilities for variation and improvisation. But always use high quality bread, which tranforms even ordinary ingredients into an extraordinary light meal or snack.

Pear and Stilton Sandwiches

8   thin slices walnut or raisin walnut bread
4   tablespoons low fat cream cheese
4   tablespoons crumbled Stilton cheese
4   tablespoons chopped walnuts
2   thinly sliced ripe but firm pears

Preheat oven to 350°.

Roast walnuts in 350° oven for 10 minutes.

Combine cream cheese and Stilton cheese with fork until well mixed. Spread on 4 slices of bread, sprinkle with walnuts and place thin slices of pear on top. Top with remaining bread slices. Cut crust off bread and cut into fourths to serve as appetizer, or serve with soup for a lovely winter lunch.

Serves 4-6

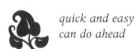 *quick and easy can do ahead*

Cucumber and Goat Cheese Tea Sandwiches

 2 medium cucumbers
 1 small onion
 1 garlic clove
 4 ounces cream cheese
 4 ounces goat cheese
 1 loaf thinly sliced bread, white or wheat

Peel cucumbers and cut lengthwise. Scoop out seeds with spoon. Salt cucumbers to draw out excess water and place over strainer for 1 hour. Rinse and dry. Slice into thin rounds.

In food processor, finely chop onion and garlic. Switch to plastic blade and add cheeses. Mix until thoroughly incorporated. Can be made 1 day ahead to this point.

Trim crusts from bread. Spread cheese mixture on slices. Top with cucumbers and second slice of bread. Cut each sandwich into 4 pieces.

Serves 15-20

 can do ahead
can freeze

Raisin Sandwiches

This sandwich is so old-fashioned it seems new.

 1 lemon, quartered and seeded, unpeeled
 1½ cups white raisins (also called golden raisins)
    mayonnaise or cream cheese to taste
 1 loaf thinly sliced wheat or white bread, crusts trimmed

Coarsely chop lemon with raisins in food processor. Refrigerate until ready to use, up to several days.

Spread bread with mayonnaise or cream cheese and top with raisin mixture. Good with cheese straws and iced tea.

Serves 20-24

 quick and easy
can do ahead

"My favorite food is a peanut butter sandwich. It tastes real good. I like it because the peanut butter sticks to my mouth."

Taylor Johnson,
first grade
Woodward student

"I served these one year at 10:00 a.m. at a Garden Club meeting and they were gone by 10:15."
Mary Collier,
Woodward parent

Chili Cream Sauce

To get the best flavor, make sauce at least several hours ahead, preferably a day before cooking and serving pork.

½ cup mayonnaise
1 cup sour cream
2 teaspoons finely chopped red peppers
¼ cup finely chopped green chilies
1 tablespoon finely chopped onion
2 teaspoons chili powder
2 teaspoons cumin
1 large garlic clove, minced
½ teaspoon lemon pepper, optional
pinch of cayenne
salt to taste

Mix ingredients together and store in airtight jar in refrigerator until ready to use.

Tangy Tenderloin Sandwiches with Chili Cream Sauce

Served warm, cold or at room temperature, these are always memorable.

2 pork tenderloins (1 package)
3 large onions, sliced in large rings
1 can beer
¼ cup water
3 tablespoons olive oil
16 2-inch round dinner rolls
chili cream sauce

Preheat oven to 350°.

Brown tenderloins in olive oil, approximately 5 minutes per side. Add onions, cover with beer and ¼ cup water. Bring to boil, lower heat, cover and simmer 15-20 minutes.

Remove tenderloins and cut into ¼-inch slices. Place in 9x13-inch glass baking dish and cover with onion and beer mixture. Bake at 350° until pork is cooked, 20-30 minutes.

Meanwhile warm rolls, slice and spread both halves with chili cream sauce. Add pork. You may want to top pork with cooked sliced onion.

Makes about 16 sandwiches

 can do ahead

Stuffed Baguette with Spinach, Ham and Walnuts

- 1 8-ounce package frozen spinach, thawed and pressed dry
- 4 ounces cream cheese
- 1 tablespoon half-and-half
- 4 cups minced ham, about 1 pound
- ⅓ cup coarsely chopped walnuts
- ⅓ cup mayonnaise
- 1 tablespoon Dijon mustard
- 1 long baguette, sliced lengthwise and hollowed out

Blend together spinach, cream cheese and half-and-half until spreadable. Set aside.

Combine ham, walnuts, mayonnaise and mustard. Set aside.

Completely coat inside surfaces of baguette with cream cheese mixture. Pack ham mixture into hollow of baguette bottom, mounding to fill hollowed top. Replace top on baguette. Wrap securely in plastic wrap.

Refrigerate at least 2 hours, or up to 8. Slice and serve.

Makes 15-20 slices

 *easy
do ahead*

Cook's Tip:

If you'd like to use fresh spinach in place of frozen, cook in covered saucepan with only the water that clings after washing. Cook about 3 minutes over medium heat until spinach is just wilted. Drain and squeeze dry. Chop and proceed with recipe as with frozen.

Cook's Tip:

If making sandwiches several hours ahead, you will want to keep bread moist and fresh. Thoroughly wet paper towel, squeeze out excess water, and place moist paper towel lightly over sandwiches. Cover with plastic wrap. This procedure will work for most sandwiches except those with particularly moist fillings.

Aunt Nell's Tomato Sandwiches

While the tomatoes take on an onion flavor, there is no raw onion in these ladylike sandwiches.

- 2 firm, vine ripe tomatoes
   salt to taste
- 1 large Vidalia onion, cut in 9 slices
- 2 tablespoons cream cheese
- 2 tablespoons mayonnaise
- 8 slices white bread, cut in rounds the size of tomato slices
- 8 slices wheat bread, cut in rounds the size of tomato slices
   black pepper

Begin the night before. Drop tomatoes in pot of boiling water for 30 seconds. Remove and peel. Slice each tomato in 4 slices. Layer with onion in airtight container. Refrigerate overnight.

Mix together cream cheese and mayonnaise.

To assemble, spread both sides of bread with cream cheese mixture. Using 1 white and 1 wheat round for each sandwich, put 1 tomato slice on top, salt to taste, and cover with other round. Crack black pepper on top of sandwiches and keep in airtight container with moist paper towel spread on top until ready to eat. (Reserve onion for other uses.)

Makes 8 sandwiches

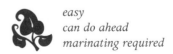

easy
can do ahead
marinating required

Country Pâté Madeira

⅓ cup butter
1 large Bermuda onion, chopped
2 cloves garlic, chopped
1 pound chicken livers, drained
1 teaspoon dried tarragon
1 teaspoon salt, or to taste
½ teaspoon black pepper
1 teaspoon dried thyme
¼ teaspoon cayenne pepper
¼ teaspoon ground cloves
¼ teaspoon allspice
¼ cup Madeira wine
1 teaspoon cracked black pepper
    sliced cornichon pickles, optional

Heat butter in large skillet. Add onions and garlic. Sauté over medium to low heat 10 minutes.

Add drained livers to onion and garlic. Sauté 7 to 10 minutes until no longer pink. Sprinkle with tarragon, salt, pepper, thyme, cayenne pepper, cloves and allspice.

Put liver mixture in food processor with chopper blade and puree until smooth. Add Madeira and process to combine. Refrigerate at least several hours, preferably 1 day ahead.

Serve at room temperature, topped with cracked black pepper. If freezing, pack in 2-quart airtight container until ready to thaw. Thaw in refrigerator 1 day before serving.

Serve on fresh bread and top with sliced cornichon pickle.

Serves 10-16

 *do ahead*
can freeze

Cook's Tip:

Place plastic wrap tightly over the pâté to avoid discoloration.

French Pâté Battistini

This is the classic pâté found in French home kitchens.

¾ pound chicken livers, halved with fibrous tissue cut off and discarded
2 cups dry or sweet vermouth
   salt and pepper to taste
1 tablespoon cooking oil
2 large shallots, minced
½ pound butter
1 dash of cayenne, optional

Marinate livers in salt, pepper and vermouth for 2 hours. Strain livers, saving marinade minus ½ cup.

Heat oil in medium skillet and sauté livers 10 minutes. Place livers in food processor or blender. Meanwhile, in same skillet, cook marinade and shallots over medium-low heat until reduced by at least half. Reducing the liquid is crucial. Let cool.

Place marinade/shallot mixture in food processor or blender with livers. Add butter and cayenne if desired. Blend gently. Spoon into bowl and refrigerate at least 4 hours, preferably overnight.

Serve with rounds of fresh French or sourdough bread.

Serves 8-10

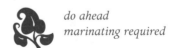

*do ahead
marinating required*

Pull Out the Stops
Smoked Salmon Pâté

12	ounces cream cheese, room temperature
4	ounces butter, room temperature
2	tablespoons sour cream
4	ounces smoked salmon, in pieces
1	tablespoon minced onion
2	teaspoons prepared horseradish
2	tablespoons domestic caviar
2	hard-boiled eggs, chopped
2	tablespoons chopped parsley

Combine and blend first 6 ingredients with hand mixer. Shape into mound and place on serving plate. Chill.

When ready to serve, sprinkle mound with caviar. Mix parsley and egg together and place in a circle around pâté.

Serves 6-8

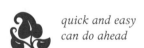 *quick and easy*
can do ahead

Cook's Tip:

Many grocery stores sell smoked salmon scraps at an appreciably lower than regular price.

Toasted Pita Triangles

4 8-inch pita
   rounds
   olive oil for
   brushing
   coarse salt
   finely chopped
   rosemary

Preheat oven to 350°.
Separate pita halves.
Brush inside surface
lightly with olive oil,
then sprinkle with
coarse salt and rose-
mary. Cut each round
into 8 triangles and
bake in 350° oven until
lightly browned and
crisp, 10-12 minutes.
These are also great
with cheese or by
themselves with drinks.

Hummus

*There are as many versions of hummus as there are cooks. Measure out
the ingredients to your own taste.*

2 cups chickpeas with 2 teaspoons liquid reserved
2 garlic cloves, crushed
3 tablespoons lemon juice, or to taste
3 tablespoons tahini, or to taste, available at most
   supermarkets
½ teaspoon ground cayenne pepper
½ teaspoon ground cumin
   salt to taste

   fresh parsley or cilantro

In food processor, blend ingredients until almost smooth. Adjust
seasonings to taste. Will keep refrigerated several days.

Garnish with parsley and cilantro. For a wonderful appetizer tray,
serve Hummus with Toasted Pita Triangles, Greek olives, feta cheese
and sliced ripe tomatoes drizzled with oil and vinegar.

Makes about 2 cups

*quick and easy
can do ahead*

Lemon Garlic Bean Dip

2 15-ounce cans black beans, drained
1 teaspoon ground cumin
2 teaspoons minced garlic
1 tablespoon safflower or canola oil
2 tablespoons red wine or rice wine vinegar
4 tablespoons chopped fresh cilantro
1 canned or pickled jalapeño pepper, seeded and minced
3 - 4 tablespoons lemon juice (about 1 lemon)

Blend all ingredients in food processor or blender until smooth. Refrigerate at least several hours for flavors to meld. Keeps in refrigerator several days.

Serve with tortilla chips, pita chips or bagel chips.

**Makes approximately
2 cups**

*quick and easy
do ahead*

Variations:

Kidney, white or red beans can be substituted for black beans. Chickpeas create a different but tasty dip.

Artichoke, Pepper and Basil Dip

Perfect when you want to eat light but do not want to feel deprived, this low fat vegetarian dip is spicy and rich tasting.

½ cup low-fat mayonnaise
½ cup no-fat sour cream
1 15-ounce can artichoke hearts, drained and chopped
⅓ cup chopped roasted red peppers
1 garlic clove, minced
2 tablespoons chopped fresh basil or 2 teaspoons dried
⅛ teaspoon dried oregano
⅛ teaspoon salt

Combine all ingredients. Place in serving dish, cover and refrigerate at least 1 hour.

Serve with wheat crackers or water wafers.

Makes 1⅔ cups

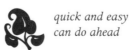
*quick and easy
can do ahead*

Variation:

Replace the roasted red peppers with roasted jalapeño peppers to create a creamy but tinglingly hot dip for tortilla chips.

Roasted Garlic

Roasting garlic gives it a mellow, nutty taste. A teaspoon stirred into soups, stews, sauces or vinaigrettes can make a good dish outstanding.
Choose hard, unblemished heads and remove any loose papery outer skin. Cut off the top ¼ inch to expose the individual cloves. Place each head in the middle of a 10-inch square of heavy duty aluminum foil, drizzle with 1 teaspoon olive oil and sprinkle with salt. Bring foil up around garlic and wrap tightly. Bake in 350° oven for 45 minutes. For more caramelized results, unwrap for the last 10 minutes of baking.
Squeeze head or individual cloves to remove the pulp. You can also serve whole roasted heads with warm slices of bread as an appetizer.

Vidalia Onion Dip

2   Vidalia onions, chopped
2   cups shredded Swiss cheese
1   cup mayonnaise
    white pepper to taste

Preheat oven to 350°.
Combine all ingredients in shallow, glass baking dish. You may refrigerate at this point until ready to proceed. Bake at 350° until top is golden brown, about 30 minutes. Serve warm with crackers or French bread rounds.

Makes about 2 cups

quick and easy

Black-Eyed Pea Salsa

1   can black-eyed peas, drained
2   medium tomatoes, chopped
1   bunch green onions, sliced
1   tablespoon chopped fresh cilantro
3   tablespoons fresh lime juice
1   tablespoon olive oil
2   garlic cloves, minced
½   teaspoon ground cumin
¼   teaspoon salt
1   tablespoon chopped jalapeño pepper

Combine all ingredients in large bowl, cover and refrigerate at least 4 hours or, even better, overnight.
Serve with tortilla chips.

Makes about 2 cups

quick and easy
do ahead

Soups
and
Salads

Soups and Salads

Menus

Butternut Tomato Bisque

2 pounds (3-4 cups) peeled and
   cubed butternut squash
3 cups chicken stock
2 large onions, chopped
1 15-ounce can of tomatoes
1 cup half-and-half
1-2 drops hot red pepper sauce
   salt and fresh black pepper to taste
½ cup heavy cream
   fresh chopped chives

Place cubed squash in large pot with stock, onions, tomatoes, salt and pepper. Simmer until vegetables are tender.

Cool. Blend well in food processor or blender, in batches if necessary.

Add half-and-half and mix well. Add hot red pepper sauce and check seasonings. (Can freeze at this point.)

Just before serving, swirl in cream and sprinkle with chopped chives.

Serve hot or cold with crisp rolls or garlic bread.

Serves 6-8

*can do ahead
can freeze*

"As a new immigrant I made this for our first Thanksgiving in America nine years ago. Now it is tradition among all our friends, both American and South African, that we have this soup at Thanksgiving."

*Franeen Sarif,
Woodward parent*

Variations:

Pumpkin can be used in place of squash. To make a lower fat version of this bisque, use 2% milk in place of half-and-half; instead of swirling in heavy cream, thin low or no-fat sour cream with 2% milk until it reaches the consistency of cream.

Cook's Tip:

While canned stock works in a pinch, homemade tastes better and is easy to keep on hand, frozen in small containers.

Basic Chicken Stock

3-4	pounds chicken wings, necks and/or backs
1	onion, peeled and quartered
1	large carrot, chopped in large pieces
1	stalk celery, chopped in large pieces
1	teaspoon salt
6-8	whole black peppercorns

Place chicken pieces in large stock pot and add water to cover by about 2 inches. Bring to gentle boil and skim off gray foam as it forms. Reduce heat and add remaining ingredients. Simmer partially covered 3-4 hours. Add water to cover as needed.

Strain stock through fine sieve and discard chicken and vegetables. Allow to cool, then refrigerate. Before using stock, lift off fat that has solidified on surface.

Refrigerated stock should be used within 2 days. Freeze for longer storage.

Makes about 2 quarts

*easy
do ahead
can freeze*

Curried Cream of Carrot Soup

½ cup butter
2 medium onions, chopped
4 tablespoons flour, sifted as incorporated
6 cups chicken stock
3 pounds carrots, peeled and chopped
¼ teaspoon curry powder or more to taste
½ pint half-and-half
   salt and black pepper to taste

Heat butter in large saucepan. Add onion. Cook over low heat about 5 minutes. Sift in flour and stir over medium heat 1 minute. Remove from heat.

Gradually stir in chicken stock, carrots and spices. Return to heat and simmer until carrots are tender, about 30 minutes. Blend in blender or food processor in batches until smooth. Season and add half-and-half. Reheat without boiling.

Serves 4

 *easy*
can do ahead

Spanish Bean Soup

2 15-ounce cans garbanzo beans, drained
½ pound ham, cubed
3 ounces dried chorizo sausage, sliced
2 bay leaves
   salt and pepper to taste
1 pinch saffron
1½ quarts water
1 onion, chopped
2 garlic cloves, chopped
¼ green pepper, chopped
2 large potatoes

Put drained beans, ham, sausage, bay leaves, salt, pepper and saffron in pot with water. Bring to boil, turn down and simmer 20 minutes.

Sauté onion, garlic and green pepper and add to soup. Cut up potatoes and add. Simmer about ½ hour longer or until potatoes are cooked.

This soup is great served with French or Cuban bread.

Serves 4-6

  easy
can do ahead

Cook's Tip:

Chorizo sausage is available both fresh and dried. Fresh sausage can be removed from its casing and browned as you would ground beef or cooked on a grill or stove-top. Dried chorizo resembles pepperoni. Used in small amounts, it adds a wonderfully smokey flavor to soups and stews. It is also great thinly sliced on pizzas.

Cajun Crab Bisque

½ cup unsalted butter
½ cup all-purpose flour
2 cups chicken broth
1 teaspoon liquid crab boil
2 cups fresh corn off the cob (4 ears)
   or may use frozen
3 cups bottled clam juice
½ pint heavy cream
1 pound canned lump crabmeat
½ tablespoon Cajun seasoning
1 teaspoon lemon pepper
1 bunch green onion, chopped
   salt and pepper to taste

In large saucepan melt butter and add flour. Cook, stirring constantly, until flour sticks to pan. Add broth and crab boil. Bring to boil, stirring constantly, then lower heat and simmer 15 minutes.

Add corn kernels and clam juice and continue simmering 15 minutes more.

Add cream and blend well. Gently add crabmeat, salt and pepper, Cajun seasoning, lemon pepper and ½ cup green onion. Remove from heat and let stand 15 minutes.

To serve, ladle bisque into bowls and top with remaining green onions.

Serves 8

 easy

Chicken Lime Soup

1	tablespoon olive oil
1	medium onion, finely chopped
1	hot green chili, minced
2	chicken breasts, cut into bite-sized pieces
3	tomatoes, peeled, seeded and chopped
8	cups chicken stock, preferably homemade
½	cup lime juice
	salt and pepper to taste

1	tomato, cut into 6 slices
3	sprigs cilantro, chopped
1	lime, cut into 6 slices

In medium to large pot, sauté onion in oil until translucent. Add chili and chicken and sauté briefly. Add tomatoes. Stir and add chicken stock. Bring to boil, then simmer, covered, until chicken is tender. Stir in lime juice and season with salt and pepper.

Serve hot soup garnished with cilantro, tomato and lime slices.

Serves 6

 *easy*
can do ahead
can freeze

> **Cook's Tip:**
>
> *To peel tomatoes, dip them in boiling water for 30 seconds, then into cold water. Loosened skin will peel away easily.*

Ginger Chicken and Corn Soup

Cook's Tip:

The flavor of fresh ginger is peppery, a little sweet and very aromatic; it is used extensively in Asian and Indian dishes. Ground ginger is used more often in American and European foods; the two cannot be used interchangeably, as the flavors are very different. Fresh, unpeeled ginger can be stored, tightly wrapped, in the refrigerator for up to a week and can be frozen up to 2 months.

2	pounds chicken pieces
10	cups water
4	black peppercorns
1	1-inch piece ginger, peeled and sliced thin
1	medium onion, peeled and quartered
3	sprigs parsley
1	teaspoon salt
2	15-ounce cans creamed corn
2	chicken bouillon cubes
½	teaspoon grated ginger
5	green onions, chopped
	salt and pepper to taste
1	teaspoon sesame oil
4	tablespoons cornstarch
6	tablespoons water, divided
2	egg whites
4	green onions, chopped

Place chicken into large saucepan. Add water, peppercorns, sliced ginger, onion, parsley and salt. Bring to a boil over medium heat. Skim well to remove any scum. Reduce heat and simmer gently, covered, for 1½ hours. Skim again. Remove chicken. Strain and reserve six cups of stock.

In large saucepan, combine reserved chicken stock, creamed corn, crumbled bouillon cubes, grated ginger, chopped green onions, salt, pepper and sesame oil. Bring to boil. Mix cornstarch with 4 tablespoons water to make smooth paste. Add to soup. Stir until soup boils and thickens. Reduce heat. Simmer 1-2 minutes.

Lightly beat egg whites and 2 tablespoons water. Add to soup in thin stream, stirring well.

Remove chicken meat from bones and shred. Add 1 cup shredded chicken to soup. Heat gently.

Garnish with chopped green onions.

Serves 6-8

*easy
can do ahead*

Corn Chowder with Bacon

10 slices bacon
 1 medium yellow onion, chopped
 2 large baking potatoes, diced
¾ cup water
 2 15-ounce cans creamed corn
15 ounces whole kernel corn, fresh, canned or frozen
 3 cups 2% milk
 3 tablespoons butter
¼ cup finely chopped fresh parsley
    salt and black pepper to taste

Cook bacon until crisp. Crumble and set aside. Reserve drippings.

In about 2 tablespoons bacon drippings, sauté onion until lightly browned. Add diced potatoes and water. Cook on medium-low heat until potatoes are just tender, about 15 minutes.

Add half the crumbled bacon, both corns, milk, butter, parsley, salt and pepper. Simmer gently, 30-40 minutes, to desired thickness.

Ladle into serving bowls and garnish with remaining crumbled bacon.

Serves 8-10

easy
can do ahead

Menu

Tailgate Picnic

Corn Chowder
with Bacon
47

Stuffed Baguette
with Spinach,
Ham and Walnuts
31

Smoked Edam and
Basil Marinated
Tomatoes
56

Raspberry Bars
209

Hot and Sour Shrimp Soup

Variation:

Instead of shrimp, try 1½ cups chopped chicken.

Cook's Tip:

If a recipe calls for arrowroot and you don't have it, you can always use an equal amount of cornstarch.

Cook's Tip:

Tofu, also called soybean curd, is made from the liquid extracted from cooked, ground soybeans. It has very little flavor of its own and readily takes on the flavor of anything in which it is marinated or with which it is cooked. Tofu is a good source of protein while being cholesterol free. It has also been implicated in the lower incidence of breast cancer in Asian countries where a great deal of tofu and other soy-based foods are consumed.

3   cups chicken broth
1   tablespoon fresh lemon juice
1   cup thinly sliced fresh mushrooms
4   ounces tofu, drained and cut in ½-inch disks
1   tablespoon arrowroot mixed with ¼ cup water
1½   tablespoons rice vinegar
1½   tablespoons sweet sake or sherry
1½   tablespoons soy sauce
    hot pepper sauce to taste
2   teaspoons fresh ginger or to taste
½   cup raw shrimp, peeled, deveined and chopped
½   cup thinly sliced celery

3   tablespoons chopped green onions and/or chopped cilantro to taste

Bring chicken broth and lemon juice to boil in medium pot. Simmer a few minutes. Add mushrooms and tofu. Bring to a boil. Stir in arrowroot mixed with water to lightly thicken. Add vinegar, soy sauce, sake, hot sauce and ginger. Simmer 5 minutes.

Add shrimp and celery and cook a few minutes more until shrimp just turns pink. Celery should remain crisp. Pour into bowls and garnish with green onion and cilantro.

Serves 4

Buttermilk Gazpacho

A refreshing change from the more traditional versions.

3-4	large fresh tomatoes, coarsely chopped
1¼	cups tomato juice
1	cup buttermilk, no-fat okay
1	Vidalia onion, coarsely chopped
1	small cucumber, coarsely chopped
1	small green pepper, coarsely chopped
1	clove garlic
2	tablespoons olive oil
1	teaspoon chili powder
½	teaspoon salt
½	teaspoon cumin
½	teaspoon hot pepper sauce

sour cream or yogurt to taste

Combine all ingredients in large mixing bowl.

Place half in blender or food processor and process until almost smooth. Repeat with remaining half, but only process until chunky. Combine and chill. May top with a dollop of sour cream or yogurt.

Serves 6-8

 *quick and easy can do ahead*

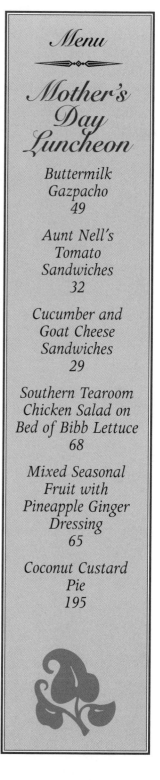

Menu

Mother's Day Luncheon

Buttermilk
Gazpacho
49

Aunt Nell's
Tomato
Sandwiches
32

Cucumber and
Goat Cheese
Sandwiches
29

Southern Tearoom
Chicken Salad on
Bed of Bibb Lettuce
68

Mixed Seasonal
Fruit with
Pineapple Ginger
Dressing
65

Coconut Custard
Pie
195

Variation:

Substituting vegetable broth for chicken broth turns this bisque into a delicious vegetarian choice.

Summer Vegetable Bisque

2 tablespoons butter
1 cup chopped onion
4 heaping cups summer vegetables of choice (squash, zucchini, broccoli, cauliflower or asparagus)
4 cups chicken broth
½ teaspoon sugar
½ teaspoon salt
¼ teaspoon white pepper
1 cup half-and-half, optional

Melt butter and sauté onion in medium stock pot. Add vegetables, chicken broth, sugar, salt and pepper. Bring to boil and cook on moderate heat until tender, about 20 minutes. Remove from heat and puree soup in blender. Return to pot and add half-and-half, if desired. Heat gently. Serve hot or cold.

Serves 6-8

 *easy
can do ahead*

Cold and Spicy Tomato Soup

5-6	medium garlic cloves, minced
2½	teaspoons sweet paprika
1½	teaspoons cumin
	pinch of cayenne pepper
4	teaspoons olive oil
2¼	pounds Italian plum tomatoes, peeled and seeded
¼	cup chopped fresh cilantro, leaves only
1	tablespoon white wine vinegar
2	tablespoons plus 2 teaspoons fresh lemon juice
3	tablespoons water
2	stalks celery, finely diced
	salt to taste

In small saucepan over low heat, stir together garlic, paprika, cumin, cayenne and olive oil. Cook 2 minutes, stirring constantly. Remove from heat and set aside.

In food processor or blender, puree cold tomatoes to thin consistency. Stir in cooked spice mixture and remaining ingredients. Refrigerate until well chilled. Best made a day ahead.

Serves 4

 *freezes*
can do ahead

Cook's Tip:

To decorate any soup, you can thin no-fat sour cream or yogurt with stock to equal the soup's consistency, place in a ziplock bag, snip off a tiny corner and drizzle decoratively over soup.

Cook's Tip:

Using tepid water to wash greens will help remove grit easier.

Mixed Greens With a Bouquet of Dressings

Sometimes nothing will do but a simple green salad well dressed.

Bibb lettuce
romaine lettuce
radicchio
arugula

Mix lettuces in equal amounts and toss with one of the following dressings. Or serve dressings separately, offering guests a choice.

Emerald Dressing

This creamy and somewhat rich dressing is particularly good over romaine lettuce.

¼   cup vegetable oil
¼   cup olive oil
1¼ tablespoons lemon juice
¾   cup vinegar
1   garlic clove, pressed
⅓   teaspoon salt
½   cup Romano cheese
¼   cup chopped fresh parsley

Combine ingredients in blender until smooth.

Raisin Basil Vinaigrette

A light dressing, sweet yet tart.

⅓   cup raisins (golden makes dressing sweeter)
1   teaspoon minced garlic
¼   cup rice vinegar
¼   cup water
1   tablespoon canola or safflower oil
1 to 2 teaspoons lemon juice
¾   cup fresh basil leaves, chopped (about 20 large leaves) or more to taste
salt and fresh ground black pepper to taste

In blender, not food processor, mix raisins, minced garlic and vinegar until raisins are finely chopped, less than a minute. Add water, oil and lemon juice. Blend again for a few seconds. Add chopped basil and blend until rich green color. Add salt and ground pepper to taste.

Herbed French Dressing

- ½ teaspoon salt
- 1 teaspoon dried oregano leaves
- 1 teaspoon dried basil leaves
- 1 teaspoon dried tarragon leaves
- 1 teaspoon onion powder
- ½ teaspoon sugar
- ½ teaspoon garlic powder
- ½ teaspoon powdered mustard
- ⅛ teaspoon ground black pepper
- 1 cup canola or olive oil
- ¼ cup cider vinegar
- 1-2 tablespoons lemon juice

Combine first 10 ingredients and let stand at least 1 hour. Whisk in vinegar and lemon juice.

Romaine and Watercress with Tart Walnut Vinaigrette

- 1 small head torn romaine lettuce leaves
- 1 bunch watercress, tough stems removed
- ½ cup coarsely chopped toasted walnuts
- ½ cup crumbled Gorgonzola cheese
  Tart Walnut Vinaigrette

Divide greens among 6 salad plates. Top with walnuts and cheese. Spoon vinaigrette over salads.

Serves 6

quick and easy

Tart Walnut Vinaigrette

- 1 tablespoon walnut oil
- 3 tablespoons white balsamic vinegar
- 1 crushed garlic clove
- 1 tablespoon Dijon mustard
- ½ teaspoon sugar
  salt and freshly ground pepper to taste

Combine ingredients together and whisk.

Baby Blue Salad

1 pound baby lettuces
4 ounces crumbled blue cheese
3 cups balsamic vinaigrette
3 oranges, peeled and sliced
4 kiwis, peeled and sliced
1½ pints strawberries, hulled and quartered
4 ounces sweet and spicy walnuts, optional

Toss baby lettuces with balsamic vinaigrette and blue cheese, using enough dressing to coat lettuce without drowning it. Place in center of serving plate. Arrange oranges, kiwis and strawberries over lettuces and top with sweet and spicy walnuts if desired.

Serves 6

quick and easy

Eggless Caesar Salad

1-2 large heads romaine lettuce

2 garlic cloves, minced
¼ cup vegetable oil
¼ cup olive oil
    salt and fresh pepper to taste
¼ teaspoon dry mustard
3 anchovy fillets, minced
2 tablespoons lemon juice
    dash Worcestershire sauce
    red wine vinegar to taste
    garlic croutons (page 55)
    shredded Parmesan cheese

Wash romaine lettuce and tear into bite-sized pieces.

Combine ingredients for dressing and mix well. Just before serving, toss lettuce with dressing, croutons and Parmesan cheese.

Serves 4-6

quick and easy

Balsamic Vinaigrette

½ cup balsamic vinegar
2 tablespoons honey
1 tablespoon minced fresh shallots
2 tablespoons Dijon mustard
1 tablespoon fresh minced garlic
1½ cups olive oil
    salt and pepper to taste

Whisk vinegar, honey, shallots, Dijon mustard and garlic until thick. Slowly add oil while whisking. Add salt and pepper to taste.

Sweet and Spicy Walnuts

2 tablespoons sugar
1 tablespoon chili powder
2 tablespoons brown sugar
6 ounces walnut pieces
1 egg white, lightly beaten

Preheat oven to 350°.

Mix sugars and spices together. Mix nuts with egg white. Toss with sugar mixture to coat. Spread on roasting pan and roast in 350° oven until golden brown, about 10 minutes.

Spinach Salad with Water Chestnuts

2 bunches fresh spinach, cleaned, stemmed and dried
2 cups bean sprouts
⅓ cup sliced water chestnuts
⅓ cup sliced almonds, toasted
6 strips crisp, cooked bacon, crumbled
2 hard boiled eggs, sliced thin
4 green onions, sliced
1½ cups fresh sliced mushrooms

Tear spinach into bite-sized pieces. Layer salad ingredients and toss gently to coat with your choice of vinaigrette dressings.
Serves 4-6

*quick and easy
can do ahead*

Raisin Bacon Broccoli Slaw

1 1-pound package broccoli slaw
1 8-ounce package shredded red cabbage
1 cup chopped broccoli flowerets
¾ cup chopped celery
¾ cup golden raisins

¾ cup mayonnaise
¼ teaspoon curry powder or to taste
¼ cup sugar or less to taste
3 tablespoons rice wine vinegar

4 slices crisp cooked bacon, crumbled
¾ cup salted, dry roasted peanuts

Mix first 5 salad ingredients together.
Mix dressing ingredients, pour over salad and toss thoroughly. Refrigerate at least 2 hours before serving.
Just before serving add peanuts and cooked bacon. Toss and serve.
Serves 8-10

*quick and easy
do ahead*

Garlic Croutons

sliced white bread
vegetable oil
garlic salt or garlic
    powder

Preheat oven to 350°. Remove crusts from bread and cut into bite-size pieces. Coat baking sheet lightly with vegetable oil and toss bread pieces in oil. Sprinkle generously with garlic salt or powder. Bake at 350° until croutons are golden brown, 10-15 minutes.

Variations:

Use flowerets instead of slaw for broccoli salad. Substitute sunflower seeds for peanuts.

Greek Salad Araim

3 ripe red tomatoes
1 medium cucumber
1 green pepper
1 onion
  salt and freshly ground pepper
  oregano to taste
1 cup black kalamata olives
½ cup feta cheese, in chunks
½ cup olive oil
¼ cup cider vinegar

Cut tomatoes, cucumber and pepper into slices. Cut onion in circles. Toss with salt and pepper and oregano. Add olives and feta. Drizzle with olive oil and vinegar to taste.

Serve with fish or lamb. This salad also makes a nice light supper or lunch served with Spanakopita (page 14) and Honey Grapes (page 213).

Serves 4-6

quick and easy

Smoked Edam and Basil Marinated Tomatoes

4 medium ripe tomatoes, quartered
8 fresh basil leaves, torn into pieces
½ cup grated smoked Edam or Gouda cheese
2 tablespoons vinaigrette
  fresh coarse pepper
  salt, optional

Lightly toss together or layer on serving plate, tomatoes, basil and cheese. Drizzle vinaigrette over salad. Salt and pepper to taste, using lots of pepper, but not much salt.

Serve chilled.

Serves 6

*quick and easy
can do ahead*

Caprece

You can eat this Tuscan tomato salad by itself or garnished with a bit of pesto.

4	vine ripe tomatoes
16	1-inch slices mozzarella cheese
16	fresh basil leaves
	extra virgin olive oil
	pesto
	salt and freshly ground pepper

On individual plates, slice each tomato, stem end down, in a fan shape. Do not cut all the way through. Place 4 slices mozzarella and 4 basil leaves in slits of tomato slices. Drizzle with olive oil.

Garnish with pesto and salt and pepper to taste.

Serves 4

 *quick and easy*

Pesto

2	cups fresh basil leaves
½	cup pine nuts
½	cup olive oil
2	garlic cloves
1	teaspoon salt
½	cup grated Parmesan cheese

In food processor combine basil, pine nuts, olive oil, garlic and salt. Scrape sides until well blended. Add cheese and process until combined.

If not using immediately, freeze pesto in ice cube trays, then pop out and store in zip lock freezer bags.

Cook's Tip:

Cutting basil leaves with a knife or scissors will cause the cut edges to blacken. When basil is to be used fresh in a salad, it will look prettier torn by hand. If you wish to cut, stack up to 10 basil leaves, roll the leaves carefully into a loose tube and slice diagonally with a sharp knife or kitchen scissors.

Cook's Tip:

Combining herbs and vegetables with olive oil requires careful and proper short term storage. While commercial garlic-in-oil mixtures are acidified to prevent bacterial growth, the University of Georgia Extension Service recommends that when such oil combinations are prepared at home, they should be refrigerated quickly and used within 3 days or else frozen.

Menu

Soup and Salad Fall Lunch

Spanish Bean Soup
43

Fresh Corn
and Sweet
Pepper Salad
58

Pear and Stilton
Cheese Sandwiches
28

Chocolate
Macadamia
Nut Pie
227

Fresh Corn and Sweet Pepper Salad

Warning: This corn salad is habit forming.

3	cups corn (6 ears fresh), or may use frozen
1	large onion, chopped
2	medium zucchini, peeled and cubed
1	bunch green onion, chopped
1	sweet red pepper, chopped
1	green bell pepper, chopped
¼	cup minced fresh parsley
1	garlic clove, minced
¼	teaspoon salt
⅛	teaspoon pepper
2	teaspoons sugar
1	teaspoon ground cumin
2	teaspoons Dijon mustard
¼	teaspoon hot red pepper sauce
⅔	cup vegetable oil
⅓	cup white vinegar

Cook corn, drain and cool. Combine corn with next 6 ingredients. Set aside.

Combine garlic with remaining ingredients and blend well. Toss with vegetable mixture. Chill 8 hours. Serve with slotted spoon.

Serves 12-14

 *quick and easy
do ahead
marinating required*

Black Bean Salad with Cumin Vinaigrette

Not only does this salad taste great, it's also good for you. Low in fat and sodium, it is a good source of vitamins C and A from the peppers and tomatoes while the beans provide fiber, protein, potassium and calcium.

2   15-ounce cans black beans, drained and rinsed
2   cups corn, cooked on the cob and cut off or thawed if frozen
2   cups halved cherry tomatoes
1   cup chopped red bell pepper
1   cup chopped green bell pepper
1   cup chopped green or white onion
½   cup minced fresh cilantro

3   tablespoons fresh lime juice (about 1 large lime)
1   tablespoon balsamic vinegar
2   tablespoons salad oil
1   small garlic clove, crushed
½   teaspoon cumin
½   teaspoon sugar
    salt and pepper to taste

Combine first 7 ingredients in large bowl.

Combine remaining ingredients in small bowl and whisk until well combined. Pour over salad until well coated, tossing gently to avoid breaking beans. Pour salad into serving bowl and refrigerate until ready to serve.

This salad can be made 1-2 days ahead but is best when made 1-2 hours before serving.

Serves 8-10

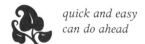

quick and easy
can do ahead

Variation:

This combination can also be served as a salsa with chips.

Sweet and Spicy Black-Eyed Pea Salad

1	cup cooked or canned black eyed peas, drained
½	cup crushed pineapple
½	red bell pepper, diced
½	red onion, diced
¾	cup pineapple juice
½	cup lime juice (about 4 limes squeezed)
½	cup chopped cilantro
2	teaspoons ground cumin
1	tablespoon minced red or green chile pepper
	salt and freshly cracked black pepper to taste

head of romaine lettuce, cleaned and torn

Mix together and serve on lettuce leaves.

Makes about 2 cups

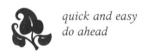 *quick and easy
do ahead*

Sweet Potato Salad

Sweet potatoes are enjoying a deserved renaissance thanks to their healthful qualities and their vivid flavor.

2	pounds sweet potatoes, similar in size
2	tablespoons white wine vinegar
3	tablespoons coarse grain or Dijon mustard
1	teaspoon sugar, or more to taste
4	teaspoons olive oil
1	cup thinly sliced celery
¼	cup finely chopped red bell pepper, yellow or green okay
¼	cup thinly sliced green onion

In vegetable steamer set over boiling water, steam sweet potatoes, covered, for 8 minutes or until potatoes just begin to soften. Run potatoes under cold water, peel and cut into ½-inch dice. Return potatoes to steamer and continue to cook until tender, but not mushy, checking frequently, about 8 minutes. Transfer to bowl.

While potatoes cook, place vinegar, mustard and sugar in blender. With blender on medium high, slowly add oil until dressing is emulsified. If no blender is available, whisk oil into vinegar mixture.

Add celery, bell peppers and green onions to potatoes. Pour dressing over warm salad and serve warm or at room temperature.

Serves 6

 easy
can do ahead

Basic Red Wine Vinaigrette

2 tablespoons
   Dijon mustard
8 tablespoons red
   wine vinegar
2 teaspoons sugar
1 teaspoon salt
1 teaspoon black
   pepper
   minced parsley
   to taste
1½ cups olive oil

Measure mustard into bowl. Whisk in vinegar, sugar, salt, pepper and parsley to taste. Continue to whisk while slowly drizzling with olive oil until mixture thickens. Adjust seasoning to taste.

Rice and Mixed Vegetable Vinaigrette

A tasty change from pasta salad, this recipe carries well to picnics, cookouts and pot lucks.

8 cups hot cooked rice
2 cups vinaigrette
1 sweet red pepper, cut into thin strips
1 green pepper, cut into thin strips
1 medium purple onion, peeled and diced
1 cup raisins
1 10-ounce package frozen green peas, thawed and blanched
¼ cup chopped fresh Italian parsley
¼ cup chopped fresh dill
½ cup pitted black olives, optional
   salt and freshly ground pepper to taste

Place rice in large mixing bowl and pour 2 cups vinaigrette into rice. Toss thoroughly. Cool to room temperature.

Add remaining ingredients and toss thoroughly. Taste, correct seasoning and add additional vinaigrette if desired.

Serve immediately, or cover and refrigerate up to 4 hours (best served day it is made). Return to room temperature before serving.

Serves 14-16

*quick and easy
can do ahead*

Greek Pasta Salad

The comment from our tester: "It's hard to describe perfection."

½   cup olive oil
½   cup Parmesan cheese
¼   cup champagne or white wine vinegar
1   teaspoon minced dried oregano
2   garlic cloves, minced
1   teaspoon Dijon mustard
    pepper to taste

1   1-pound box rotini or farfalle, cooked
½   bag fresh spinach, torn into small pieces
8   ounces crumbled feta cheese
1   bunch green onions, chopped
2   cucumbers, chopped
12 cherry tomatoes, halved
½   cup Greek olives

Mix dressing ingredients and shake well. Pour ½ of dressing over hot pasta and let cool.

Combine remaining salad ingredients in 8-quart serving bowl. Pour other ½ of salad dressing over and toss with pasta. Chill.

Serve chilled, at room temperature or slightly warm.

Serves 6

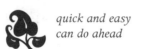

quick and easy
can do ahead

> ## Cook's Tip:
>
> *Olives produced in this country tend to be bland compared to the Niçoise olives of France or the Kalamata, Atalanti, Nafplion or green cracked olives imported from Greece. Olives should always be served at room temperature; they don't taste as good when cold. When removing olives from the jar, use tongs or a spoon to keep from introducing bacteria into the jar.*

Cook's Tip:

If preparing in advance, wait to toss in bacon until just before serving to prevent bacon from becoming soggy.

Variation:

Try a different assortment of mushrooms for slightly different flavor. You may want to sauté them briefly.

Cook's Tip:

To cut an avocado into neat slices with less mess, do not peel it first. Instead use a sharp knife to make slices through the avocado from top to bottom straight to the seed. Peel the skin off one slice at a time and, using a knife to help, remove each slice.

Variations:

This pesto sauce is delicious over tomatos or added to bean stews.

Wild Mushroom Pasta Salad

½	pound thick bacon slices
10	ounces crimini or button mushrooms, sliced
12	ounces fusilli or elbow macaroni
2	cups mayonnaise
½	cup (or more) buttermilk
1	garlic clove, crushed and minced
2	tablespoons fresh lemon juice
2	tablespoons Dijon mustard
1	tablespoon sugar
1	10-ounce package frozen peas, thawed and drained
1	bunch fresh spinach, trimmed
½	teaspoon ground red pepper or paprika, optional
	salt and pepper to taste

Cook bacon and coarsely chop. Sauté mushrooms briefly in a small portion of bacon drippings, drain and set aside. Cook pasta according to package directions.

Whisk mayonnaise, buttermilk, garlic, lemon juice, mustard and sugar in bowl. Add pasta, bacon, mushrooms and peas. Toss. Sprinkle with red pepper if desired. Season with salt and pepper. Mix well.

Can be made one day ahead. Cover and chill. Toss with more buttermilk if dry.

Line bowl with spinach leaves and fill with salad.

Serves 12

*quick and easy
do ahead*

Avocado Slices with Cilantro Pesto

2	cups packed fresh chopped cilantro
½	cup olive oil
½	teaspoon cumin
¼	cup lemon juice
2	avocados, sliced

For pesto, puree cilantro, olive oil and cumin in food processor. Slowly pour in lemon juice to form paste.

Fan avocado slices on plate and spoon dressing over.

Serves 4

*freezes
can do ahead*

Jewelled Fruit Salad

¼ cup raspberry vinegar
¾ cup walnut or olive oil
1 teaspoon Dijon mustard
2 crushed garlic cloves
1 teaspoon salt
   freshly ground black pepper to taste
8-10 large leaves, Boston or other leafy lettuce
4 cups torn romaine lettuce
1-2 red or Bartlett pears, unpeeled
1-2 kiwis, peeled
1 pint fresh raspberries
4 tablespoons crumbled blue cheese
4 tablespoons toasted walnut pieces, optional

Combine first 6 ingredients and mix well.

Place large leaves on individual salad plate. Top with torn romaine.
Arrange slices of pears and kiwi. Top with crumbled blue cheese,
raspberries and walnuts, if desired. Drizzle with vinaigrette.

Serves 4

 *quick and easy*

Strawberry Grapefruit Salad

3 tablespoons red wine vinegar
2 tablespoons unsweetened grapefruit juice
2 tablespoons vegetable oil
1 teaspoon sugar
¼ teaspoon grated grapefruit rind
⅛ teaspoon dry mustard
¼ teaspoon poppy seeds

2 cups grapefruit sections
2 cups halved strawberries
½ pound Bibb lettuce

Combine dressing ingredients, mix well and refrigerate for at least 3
hours.

Combine fruits with dressing and serve on greens.

Serves 10-12

quick and easy
marinating required

Pineapple Ginger Dressing

To give your fruit salad a slightly different flavor, omit the blue cheese and drizzle with this tangy dressing.

½ cup unsweetened crushed pineapple
¼ cup red wine vinegar
1 small garlic clove, chopped
3 tablespoons diced crystallized ginger or 3 teaspoons diced peeled ginger plus 1 tablespoon sugar
2 tablespoons pineapple juice
2 tablespoons canola oil
2 tablespoons water

In blender, blend pineapple, vinegar and garlic. Add ginger and juice. Blend again to mince ginger. Add oil and water. Blend. Refrigerate.

Warm Steak with Greens and Ginger Sauce

The contrast of warm steak over cool salad greens is lovely.

    4   ounces beef tenderloin, cut in strips
        dash ground ginger
        dash dried chili flakes
        dash teriyaki sauce
    3   tablespoons vegetable oil

    1   tablespoon vegetable oil
    1   teaspoon chopped fresh garlic
    ½   teaspoon chopped fresh ginger
    ½   teaspoon chopped dried chili flakes
    ¼   cup teriyaki sauce
    ½   cup chicken stock
    ¼   cup dry sherry (not cooking sherry which has added
        salt)
    1   teaspoon cornstarch dissolved in 2 tablespoons water
        assorted salad greens

Season beef with ginger, chili and teriyaki sauce. Heat 2 tablespoons vegetable oil in wok or sauté pan and quickly stir fry beef. Remove and keep warm.

To make ginger sauce, heat 1 tablespoon vegetable oil and add garlic, ginger and chili. Sauté 1 minute over medium high heat. Add teriyaki sauce, chicken stock and sherry. Bring to boil. Lower heat and simmer uncovered 5-6 minutes, then add cornstarch to thicken. Strain, retaining liquid as sauce.

Arrange salad greens and beef decoratively on platter. Drizzle with ginger sauce and serve.

Serves 4

 *quick and easy*

Tuna and Marinated Peppers Salad

1 red pepper
1 green pepper
1 yellow pepper
1 small red onion, thinly sliced
1 cup vinaigrette
1 12¼-ounce can tuna, drained
¼ cup mayonnaise or to taste
2 tablespoons sweet pickle relish
8 cups mixed salad greens (any combination of Bibb, romaine, iceberg or your choice)

Halve, core and thinly slice peppers. Toss with onion and vinaigrette. Let marinate in refrigerator at least 30 minutes or up to 1 week.

Combine tuna, mayonnaise and pickle relish.

On each of 4 salad plates, place about 2 cups salad greens. Top with marinated peppers and tuna salad. Spoon over Sweet-and-Sour Garlic Dressing.

Serves 4

easy
can do ahead
marinating required

Sweet-and-Sour Garlic Dressing

¼ cup vegetable oil
3 tablespoons sugar
1 rounded tablespoon spicy brown mustard
½ cup rice vinegar
1 tablespoon poppy seeds
1 tablespoon fresh lemon juice
2 tablespoons water
1 large garlic clove, chopped

Place ingredients in blender and blend on high speed for 20-30 seconds to puree garlic. Will store in refrigerator for several weeks.

Variations:

The possible additions to this basic recipe are endless. A few combinations you might try include:

* ¾ cup green grapes and ⅓ cup pecan pieces

* ½ teaspoon curry powder added to mayonnaise, about ⅔ cup mandarin orange sections added to chicken and ¼ cup sliced toasted almonds as topping

* 3 tablespoons capers, 1 tablespoon caper juice and ¼ - ⅓ cup chopped water chestnuts.

Southern Tearoom Chicken Salad

Soothing, old fashioned comfort food — sometimes nothing else will do.

3 cups diced, cooked white meat of chicken
1 cup diced celery
1 teaspoon salt or to taste
1 cup mayonnaise
1 tablespoon lemon juice
½ teaspoon paprika or to taste
  lettuce leaves, washed and separated

Combine all ingredients except lettuce and mix well. Chill for 2 hours or overnight. Arrange on lettuce leaves and sprinkle with extra paprika. Serve in sandwiches, as filling for hors d'oeuvre popovers (page 250) or on rolls with lettuce and sliced tomatoes. You could also use chicken salad to stuff avocado or tomato halves.

Serves 8-10

easy
do ahead

Buffalo Style Chicken Salad

This is no salad for dieters, but it does turn that occasional craving for greasy wings and celery dipped in little plastic cups of cheesy dressing into something elegantly delicious.

	peanut oil for frying
6	celery stalks, from the inner white stalks
4	boneless chicken breasts, cut into strips
2	tablespoons unsalted butter, room temperature
¼	teaspoon cayenne pepper
2	teaspoons lemon juice
2	teaspoons chopped fresh parsley
½	teaspoon hot pepper sauce, or to taste
	salt and pepper to taste
8	cups assorted lettuces
2	tomatoes, seeded and diced
½	cup celery leaves, from the heart
1	cup blue cheese dressing

Wash celery stalks and cut into sticks, about 2½ inches long and ¼ inch thick. Keep chilled.

Preheat peanut oil in fryer or heavy pot on high heat to 375˚.

Place chicken strips in hot oil and cook until very crisp, about 5 minutes, stirring occasionally to prevent sticking.

Combine butter, cayenne, lemon juice, parsley, hot pepper sauce, salt and pepper. Using slotted spoon, remove cooked chicken from pot and place directly in butter mixture. Toss to coat chicken evenly with butter mixture.

Toss lettuces and divide among four plates. Arrange eight chicken pieces and celery sticks on each plate, then sprinkle each salad with tomatoes and celery leaves.

Drizzle salads with blue cheese dressing. Serve remaining dressing on side.

Serves 4

Blue Cheese Dressing

⅓	cup blue cheese
2	tablespoons hot water
⅓	cup mayonnaise
⅓	cup sour cream
¼	teaspoon freshly ground black pepper
	few drops hot pepper sauce

Crumble cheese into bowl and add hot water. Mix with wooden spoon until somewhat smooth. Add mayonnaise, sour cream, pepper and pepper sauce. Refrigerate until needed. Makes about 1 cup.

Shrimp and Watercress Salad

- 1 bunch watercress, washed and dried, stems removed
- 1 large red onion, thinly sliced
- 1 pound medium-jumbo shrimp, cooked and shelled
- 2 hard-cooked eggs, sliced
- 1-2 tablespoons capers
- ½ cup crumbled feta cheese

- 2½ tablespoons Dijon mustard
- ½ cup fresh lemon juice
- ¼ cup red wine vinegar
- 2 garlic cloves, finely chopped
- ¾ cup olive oil
- 4 tablespoons chopped fresh thyme or basil
  hot pepper sauce
  salt and fresh pepper to taste

Place watercress on large platter or individual plates. Scatter circles of red onion on top, then shrimp. Intersperse with eggs, then sprinkle on capers and feta cheese.

To make dressing, mix together mustard, lemon juice, vinegar, garlic and oil. Season to taste with herbs, hot sauce, salt and pepper.

Pour dressing over salad just before serving.

Serves 5

 *easy*
can do ahead

Chilies, Curries, Casseroles and Stews

Chilies, Curries, Casseroles and Stews

White Chicken Chili for a Crowd

This light alternative to standard chili is deliciously southwestern in flavor. The longer it simmers, the better. It is even tastier the next day.

1	pound (2 cups) navy beans, soaked overnight and drained or "quick soaked"
10	cups chicken broth
2	garlic cloves, minced
2	medium onions, chopped and divided
1	tablespoon oil
2	4-ounce cans green chilies, sliced
3	cups canned quartered tomatoes, with juice
2	teaspoons ground cumin
¼	teaspoon cayenne pepper
1½	teaspoons oregano
¼	teaspoon ground cloves
4	cups diced cooked chicken, salted to taste

grated Monterey Jack cheese
chopped green onion

Combine beans, broth, garlic and half the onions in large pot and bring to boil. Simmer until beans are soft, 1 to 2 hours.

In skillet, sauté remaining onions in oil until tender. Add to pot along with chilies, tomatoes with juice and seasonings.

Add chicken and simmer 1 hour or longer. Chili can be refrigerated for 1-2 days at this point. Heat through before serving.

Garnish with cheese and green onion.

Serves 16

easy
can do ahead
can freeze

Cook's Tip:

To quick soak dried beans or peas, place in a large pot and cover with water by 2 inches. Bring water to boil, turn off heat, cover pot and let stand 1 hour. Drain.

Red Chicken Chili

Though rich in flavor, this is much lighter that you'd expect a chili to be.

Variation:

If you are in the mood for a quick stew instead of chili, cook in the microwave as follows.
In a 2-quart casserole dish, combine the onion, bell pepper, garlic and oil. Cover and microwave until softened, 3 to 4 minutes on high. Add beans with liquid and rest of ingredients. Mix well, cover and microwave for 7 minutes on high. Reduce power to low and microwave 10 to 15 minutes. Stir once or twice during cooking. Serve hot.

1	teaspoon vegetable oil
1	medium onion, diced
½	red bell pepper, cored, seeded and diced
1	garlic clove, minced
1	15-ounce can black beans with liquid
2	cups chopped fresh tomatoes
1	cup tomato sauce
1	cup frozen whole kernel corn, thawed
¼	teaspoon freshly ground black pepper
½	teaspoon salt
½	teaspoon dry mustard
1	tablespoon cumin
2	teaspoons chili powder or to taste
2	tablespoons red wine vinegar
2	teaspoons Worcestershire sauce
1½	teaspoons brown sugar
1	cup chopped cooked chicken

Heat oil in 2-quart pot. Sauté onion, pepper and garlic in oil until tender. Add rest of ingredients and simmer at least one hour.

Serves 4

 *easy*
do ahead
can freeze

Cosmic Cowboy Chili

This award winning recipe makes a very hot chili. For less incendiary results, reduce the amounts of chili powder, cayenne, hot pepper sauce and jalapeño peppers.

3	pounds ground beef or venison
2-4	medium onions
2	garlic cloves, finely chopped
1	bell pepper, red or green, finely chopped
1	16-ounce can tomato sauce
1	16-ounce can whole tomatoes
2-4	tablespoons chili powder or to taste
3	teaspoons ground cumin
2	teaspoons ground oregano
2	bay leaves
1	teaspoon red cayenne pepper
45	drops hot red pepper sauce
⅓	cup jalapeño peppers, sliced, or to taste
2	16-ounce cans dark red kidney beans

chopped red onion
shredded Monterey Jack cheese
sliced jalapeño peppers

Brown meat with onions and garlic. Place in crock pot with rest of ingredients and cook at low 4-6 hours. Or simmer ingredients in large Dutch oven, covered, at very low temperature for at least 2 hours.

Serve with one or more of the following as garnish—chopped red onion, shredded Monterey Jack cheese or sliced jalapeño peppers.

This is better served a day after cooking.

Serves 6-8

 *easy*
do ahead
can freeze

Garam Masala

Garam masala, a combination of spices used in Indian cooking, is available in many stores, but you can make your own. It stores indefinitely in an airtight container.

1 tablespoon ground cardamom or coriander
1½ teaspoons cinnamon
½ teaspoon cumin
½ teaspoon ground cloves
1 teaspoon black pepper
½ teaspoon nutmeg

Variation:

To make spicier, add 1 teaspoon curry powder.

Kheema Matar

This Indian dish of ground meat and peas brings simple ingredients to life. It can be served hot or at room temperature.

2 tablespoons vegetable oil
1 large onion, finely chopped
2 garlic cloves, chopped
1¼ inch piece of gingeroot, peeled and minced
1½ pounds lean ground turkey or beef
3 tablespoons plain yogurt
1 cup chopped fresh or canned tomatoes with liquid
2 teaspoons ground coriander
1 teaspoon ground cumin
½ teaspoon ground turmeric
¼ teaspoon cayenne, or more to taste
¼ teaspoon garam masala
2 tablespoons tomato puree
1 teaspoon salt
1 cup frozen green peas
1 cup water

Heat oil in large, deep skillet over moderate heat. Add onion and cook until onion is pale gold. Add garlic and ginger. Sauté one more minute. Crumble in ground meat. Cook three more minutes or until meat is browned.

Add yogurt, tomatoes, ground spices, tomato puree and salt. Stir well for 1 minute. Turn heat to low, cover and cook 10 minutes.

Uncover pan, turn heat to medium, add peas and water. Bring to boil, then reduce heat until mixture bubbles gently. Cook until most of the liquid has evaporated, about 15 to 20 minutes. The dish should have a small quantity of gravy but not be runny. At this point kheema can be frozen in sealed casserole dish, refrigerated for up to 2 days before serving, or served immediately over basmati rice, accompanied by fruit salad.

Serves 4

can do ahead
can freeze

Prawn and Potato Curry

The sauce for this curry is mouth-watering.

- 2 tablespoons vegetable oil
- 2 onions, finely chopped
- 2 garlic cloves, minced
- 1 cup finely chopped fresh cilantro
- 1 teaspoon salt
- 2 teaspoons garam masala
- 1 teaspoon ground turmeric
- 2 teaspoons chili powder, or to taste
- 6 tomatoes, sliced
- 1 cup hot water
- 1 pound small new potatoes, scrubbed
- 2 pounds fresh prawns (can use shrimp if prawns unavailable), peeled and deveined
- 2 teaspoons lemon juice

In large skillet, sauté onions and garlic in vegetable oil until transparent. Add cilantro and sauté gently. Add salt, garam masala, turmeric and chili powder. Cook, stirring, for 2 minutes.

Add tomatoes. Cook for 3 minutes, stirring occasionally and shaking pan. Add hot water. Bring to boil. Reduce heat to medium and cook, uncovered, for 15 minutes or until slightly thickened.

Meanwhile, steam potatoes for 10-15 minutes or until tender. Halve or quarter, depending on preference. Set aside and keep warm.

Add prawns and lemon juice to tomato mixture. Increase heat to medium-high. Cover and cook for 3-5 minutes or until prawns are pink. Add potatoes and serve immediately.

Serves 6

Goan Raita

A cooling side dish for Indian curries or any spicy dish

- 1 cucumber, peeled and finely chopped
- 2 cups yogurt
- ½ teaspoon salt
- 1 teaspoon sugar
- 2 pinches white pepper
- ¼ teaspoon ground cumin
- ¼ teaspoon ground coriander

  cilantro leaves
  a few slivers of onion

Mix all ingredients well. Serve in a decorated bowl ringed with fresh cilantro leaves and with onion slivers on top.

Variation:

You can omit the potatoes and serve the prawn curry with basmati rice.

Vegetable Curry

2	tablespoons oil
2	medium onions, cut into 1-inch dice
1	bell pepper, cut into 1-inch dice
2	cups chopped tomatoes
3-4	garlic cloves, crushed
	salt and freshly ground pepper to taste
1½	cups diced potato
1	cup sliced mushrooms
1	10-ounce package frozen peas
1	teaspoon ground turmeric
1	teaspoon chili powder
1	teaspoon ground coriander
1	teaspoon ground cumin
½	teaspoon ground cinnamon
6-8	cardamom pods

fresh cilantro
yogurt

In large skillet, sauté onion and bell pepper in oil until they begin to brown, about 10 minutes. Add tomatoes, garlic, salt and pepper. Cook five minutes. Add remaining ingredients and cover. Lower heat and simmer 45 minutes to 1 hour. Add small amounts of water as needed to prevent mixture from drying out. Can be made a day or two ahead and refrigerated, then reheated.

Serve over rice. Garnish with chopped cilantro and yogurt.

Serves 8

easy
can do ahead

Curry with Chicken and Apples

2 tablespoons clarified butter or olive oil
4 boneless, skinless chicken breast halves, cut into
   1-inch pieces
1 medium onion, chopped
3 garlic cloves, chopped
1-3 tablespoons hot Madras curry powder, to taste
2 cups chicken broth
3 bay leaves
1 ripe banana, chopped
1 medium apple, cored and chopped
½ 6-ounce can tomato paste
   raisins, shredded coconut, peanuts, sliced avocado

Heat oil in large skillet and sauté chicken pieces until browned, turning occasionally. Remove chicken and drain on paper towels.

Sauté onion and garlic in same skillet until onion is translucent. Add curry powder, broth, bay leaves, banana, apple and tomato paste. Bring to boil, lower heat, cover and simmer 20 minutes. Remove bay leaves and discard. Puree mixture in blender or food processor.

Return puree to skillet. Add cooked chicken and heat through. Serve chicken and curry sauce over cooked rice.

Pass bowls of raisins, coconut, peanuts, sliced avocado and any other condiment you like to top curry as each diner prefers.

Serves 4 generously

 easy

Ghee

Many Indian recipes call for clarified butter or "ghee." Ghee adds a rich, nutty flavor. It also has a high smoking point which makes it practical for sautéing and frying. Ghee can be purchased from Indian grocers. To make your own ghee, melt 1 pound unsalted butter in a small pot over low heat. Simmer gently for 10-30 minutes. As soon as the white residue turns to golden particles, strain the ghee through several layers of cheese cloth, cool and pour into a clean jar with a cover. Ghee will last, refrigerated, 6 months to a year.

Fried Plantains

Unlike its cousin the banana, the plantain cannot be eaten raw, nor is it sweet. These resemble potato chips.

2-3 yellow (ripe)
plantains
cooking oil
salt and pepper
to taste
hot red pepper
sauce

Remove skins from plantains. Cut crosswise in ¼-inch slices. Fry in oil until golden brown, turning to other side when edges appear brown. Watch carefully since they brown quickly. Drain on paper towels, season with salt, pepper and hot red pepper sauce to taste and serve hot.

Chicken Korma

8 ounces plain yogurt
½ teaspoon turmeric
1 teaspoon ground coriander
1 tablespoon minced fresh ginger
6 garlic cloves, minced
1 teaspoon paprika
½ teaspoon curry powder
    salt to taste
1 2-3-pound chicken, cut up and skinned or 6 chicken legs or breasts, each cut in half and skinned, or an equal amount of boneless, skinless chicken breasts
½ cup vegetable oil
1 1-inch cinnamon stick
2 whole cloves
2 whole black peppercorns
2 whole cardamom pods
1 medium onion, thinly sliced

Combine first 8 ingredients and use to marinate chicken 4 hours or overnight.

Heat oil in large saucepan or Dutch oven over high heat. Add cinnamon, cloves, peppercorns and cardamom pods. Sauté 1 minute. When slightly brown, add onion slices. Cook about 10-15 minutes until golden brown. Watch carefully to avoid burning.

Add marinated chicken pieces with sauce and continue cooking, stirring constantly. Lower heat to medium if chicken begins to stick to pan. Continue stirring.

Test chicken with fork. When chicken is almost cooked, add ¼ cup hot water and simmer over low/medium heat 10 minutes. If chicken needs more cooking, add another ½ cup hot water and simmer 20 minutes.

Turn off heat and let stand 10 minutes away from range.

Serve with rice and/or naan bread (page 251).

Serves 4-6

 *marinating required*

Jamaican Curried Chicken

Pretty enough for a party, easy enough for a week night

1   4-pound chicken, cut up
1   lime, squeezed for juice
    salt and pepper
4   tablespoons curry powder
3   tablespoons butter
2   onions, chopped
1   garlic clove, chopped
2   tomatoes, chopped
4   slices hot pepper, seeds removed
1   cup water
1   large potato cut in small chunks and placed in cold
    water until needed

Wash chicken and rub with lime juice. Season well with salt, pepper and curry powder.

Melt butter in large pot. Add chicken, onions, garlic, tomatoes and hot pepper. Pour in water and stir. Bring to boil, then lower heat to medium low, cover, and simmer 15 minutes, stirring occasionally. Add drained potatoes. Continue to simmer until gravy is formed, about 45 minutes. Gravy will not be thick.

Serve with Saffron and Red Pepper Rice (page 111), fried plantains and salad.

Serves 4-6

can do ahead
can freeze

Variation:

If you prefer a thicker gravy, combine 1 teaspoon of flour or cornstarch with 3 tablespoons of gravy in small dish. Mix well and return to curry.

Cook's Tip:

Couscous looks like rice but is actually a tiny Mediterranean pasta. It is a wonderful addition to your pantry shelf for emergency Wednesday night suppers because it requires almost no cooking.

Variations:

For a slightly different flavor, you can replace zucchini with sautéed eggplant slices. Pinenuts also make a nice addition. For a very low-fat meal, skip the butter in the couscous mixture. Simply add turmeric to couscous, raisins and boiling water.

Couscous with Chicken and Vegetables

Don't let the number of ingredients scare you. This Mediterranean staple is easy to prepare and a good bet for casual entertaining.

2	tablespoons olive oil
4	boneless, skinless chicken breast halves, cut into 1-inch pieces
2	carrots, peeled and sliced into "coins"
2	onions, sliced
3	garlic cloves, peeled and sliced
8-10	whole mushrooms, washed and stems removed
2	teaspoons ground coriander
1	teaspoon or 1 cube chicken bouillon
4-5	dried red chili peppers or dried red pepper flakes to taste
¼	teaspoon turmeric
1	cup water
2	yellow or green zucchini, sliced into ¼-inch "coins"
1	cup canned garbanzo beans, rinsed and dried
2	cups couscous
¾	cup raisins
1½	cups boiling water
¼	cup butter
¾	teaspoon turmeric

Heat oil in heavy skillet. Brown chicken pieces, remove and drain on paper towels. Refrigerate chicken if meal will be served more than 1 hour later.

To oil remaining in skillet, add carrots, onions, garlic, mushrooms, coriander, bouillon, red pepper and turmeric. Pour water over all, heat to boiling, lower heat, cover and simmer ½ hour.

Meanwhile, mix couscous, raisins and boiling water in large bowl. Cover and let stand 5 minutes, then uncover and fluff with fork. Melt butter in skillet and add turmeric. Add couscous mixture and heat through.

To vegetables in skillet, add zucchini, garbanzo beans and chicken. Simmer to heat through.

Serve chicken and vegetables in broth over couscous.

Serves 4-6

*easy
can partially do ahead*

Stuffed Eggplant Mozzarella

3 large (8 to 10-inch long) eggplants
2 tablespoons olive oil
2 cups minced onion
½ pound chopped mushrooms
2 teaspoons dried basil
⅛ teaspoon dried thyme
1 teaspoon dried oregano
1 teaspoon salt
   black pepper to taste
5 large garlic cloves, minced
2 cups cooked brown rice
2 cups grated part skim mozzarella cheese
⅛ teaspoon hot red pepper sauce
2 tablespoons soy sauce
   paprika

   minced fresh parsley

Preheat oven to 375°.

Cut eggplants in half lengthwise. Scoop out insides with ice cream scooper, leaving ½-inch shell. Mince eggplant insides into pulp. Set aside shells and pulp.

Heat oil in large skillet. Sauté onion, mushrooms and herbs over medium heat for 5 minutes. Add eggplant pulp and cook until tender, about 15 minutes. Add garlic and sauté 1 minute more. Remove from heat.

Add rice, cheese, hot red pepper sauce and soy sauce to eggplant mixture and stir well. Add additional seasonings to taste.

Place eggplant shells in large, lightly greased casserole dish and fill with mixture. They can be refrigerated at this point until ready to proceed. Bake in 375° oven 40 minutes, or until mixture is heated through and shells are tender. Sprinkle with minced fresh parsley.

Serves 6

 can do ahead

Cook's Tip:
If you have doubts when to peel eggplant, keep the following rule in mind: if cooking the eggplant a short time, peel; if cooking the eggplant a long time, do not peel.

Vegetarian Chili Relleno Casserole Sanchez

This will be as spicy as the chilies you use.

3   7-ounce cans whole green chilies
1   pound Monterey Jack cheese
1   pound longhorn cheddar cheese
3   eggs
3   tablespoons flour
1   small can evaporated milk
1   7-ounce can tomato sauce

Preheat oven to 350°.

Wash and split chilies. Remove seeds. Lay flat on paper towels to dry. Grate cheeses together, setting aside ½ cup of combined cheeses.

Place 1 layer of chilies flat in lightly greased 9x13-inch baking pan. Layer with half of grated cheese mix. Repeat with second layer of chilies and cheese.

Beat eggs, flour and evaporated milk together, then pour over dish. Bake at 350° for 30 minutes. Remove from oven, but leave oven on. Pour tomato sauce evenly over top and sprinkle with reserved ½ cup of combined cheeses. Then bake again for 15 minutes.

Cut in squares to serve, accompanied by large salad. Or cut in small wedges as appetizer or side dish with barbeque chicken or grilled steak.

Serves 8-12

 easy

> *"I put this on a crust and submitted it for the Pillsbury Bake-Off. I still think it should have won. Must have been an oversight."*
>
> *Missy Sanchez, Woodward college counselor*

Tamale Pie

 2 teaspoons olive oil
 2 large garlic cloves, pressed
 ¾ cup diced onion
 1 pound very lean ground beef
 ¾ cup diced bell pepper
 ½ teaspoon dried oregano
 1½ teaspoons cumin, or more to taste
 1 teaspoon chili powder, or more to taste
 ¼ teaspoon black pepper
 ⅛ teaspoon crushed red pepper, or more to taste
 2 cups (1-pound can) chopped tomatoes
 1½ cups yellow cornmeal
 2¾ cups cold water
 1¼ cups boiling water
 1-1½ teaspoons salt or to taste
 2 tablespoons dried minced onions
 1 tablespoon butter

sour cream, chopped green onion, chunky salsa, grated
Monterey Jack cheese, chopped fresh tomatoes

Preheat oven to 375°

In heavy skillet, sauté garlic and onion. Add ground beef and brown.
Add next 7 ingredients. Simmer, uncovered, about 20 minutes or until
liquid has evaporated. Remove from heat and set aside. Can do ahead to
this point and refrigerate 1-2 days.

In saucepan, mix cornmeal with cold water and stir well to prevent
lumps. Gradually add boiling water and stir well. Add minced onion,
butter and salt and cook over medium high heat, stirring constantly
until mixture thickens, about 3 minutes. Do not overcook; cornmeal
mixture needs to be consistency of cooked grits or porridge, but
not soupy.

Spread ½ cornmeal mixture over bottom of greased 10x6x2-inch baking
dish. Add meat and tomato mixture, smoothing with spatula to cover
uniformly. Cover meat mixture with remaining cornmeal mixture. Bake
in 375° oven until corn meal is lightly browned on top, 30-40 minutes.

Like lasagna, tamale pie needs to set up for a few minutes before
cutting to serve. Add toppings or pass individually.

Serves 4-6

 can partially do ahead

Homemade Instant Taco Mix

Use this mix in chilies, tacos, fajitas, enchiladas, or even rice dishes for extra zip.

 2 teaspoons chili powder
 ½-1 teaspoon light salt
 1-2 teaspoons cumin
 1 teaspoon flour
 ½ teaspoon garlic powder
 ½ teaspoon onion powder
  pinch of cayenne powder

Mix the ingredients together and store in airtight container.

Makes enough for 1 pound of meat.

Variation:

This meat filling is also excellent inside flour or corn taco shells.

Cranberry Cobblestone Chicken Pie

Variation:

If you omit the cranberries, you still have a nice chicken pot pie, but do not roll the crust as thin.

3 tablespoons butter
½ cup chopped celery
½ cup chopped bell pepper
¼ cup chopped onion
⅓ cup slivered almonds, optional
4 tablespoons flour, divided
1¾ cups chicken broth
½ teaspoon poultry seasoning
  salt and freshly ground pepper to taste
3 cups chopped, cooked chicken or turkey
1 cup fresh cranberries, chopped fine
¼ cup sugar
1 pie crust (page 195)
1 egg, beaten with 1 tablespoon water

Preheat oven to 350°.

Sauté celery, onion, bell pepper and almonds, if desired, in butter until onions are tender and almonds are beginning to brown. Sprinkle 3 tablespoons flour over mixture, cook and stir for 2-3 minutes. Add broth and seasonings and cook, stirring constantly, until thickened. Add chopped chicken and turn into 10-inch deep dish pie plate.

Combine chopped cranberries with sugar and remaining tablespoon flour.

Prepare pie crust and divide in half. Roll each half out on wax paper into an 11-inch round. It should be very thin, about ⅛ to 1/16 inch. Spread cranberry mixture out onto one dough circle and top with second circle. Seal by pressing edges together. Using the wax paper, lift dough and flip over onto chicken pie. Peel off wax paper and fold excess dough under to make a pretty edge. Make several slits in pie dough to allow steam to escape and brush with beaten egg.

Bake in 350° oven for 30-35 minutes.

Serves 6

Big Tom's Football Stew

    1   cup flour, or more as needed
    ¾   teaspoon black pepper
    2   pounds lean beef stew meat
    1   tablespoon olive oil, or more as needed
    1   quart water or more if needed
    2   teaspoons salt
    2   celery stalk tops, chopped
    1   onion, chopped
    2   cups beef stock or broth
    2   tablespoons fresh parsley
    1   teaspoon dried basil
    ½   teaspoon seasoned pepper

    3   medium potatoes, diced
    3   carrots, sliced
    1   8-ounce can tomato puree or stewed tomatoes
    ¼   cup red wine, optional
    1   12-ounce package frozen corn
    1   12-ounce package frozen peas
        salt and pepper to taste
        sourdough bread bowls available at bakeries and
        bread shops, optional

Combine flour and pepper in large plastic bag. Coat meat cubes in flour, then sauté in oil in large stock pot.

Add water and next 7 ingredients. Bring to boil, lower temperature and simmer, covered, over low heat for 3 hours.

Add potatoes, carrots, corn, tomato puree and wine. Cook covered until potatoes are tender. Add peas, salt and pepper. Cook 20 minutes longer. Can do ahead to this point, refrigerate for 1-2 days and reheat.

Cut tops off bread bowls and scoop out bread with fork. Reserve loose bread for other uses (great for croutons or breadcrumbs). Spoon stew into bread bowls and replace tops. If bread bowls unavailable, serve in regular bowls.

Serves 6-8

easy
can do ahead
can freeze

"Big Tom is my son and this is his favorite dinner. He's a line man on the varsity football team and when he comes home from practice he can smell it at the door. He loves eating it out of the bread bowls."

Marcy Allen,
Woodward parent

Cook's Tip:

To repair an over-salted soup or stew, add a sliced, peeled raw potato and simmer 10-15 minutes. Remove potato before serving.

Ed's Brunswick Stew

Perfect for feeding a crowd

2	2½-3 pound fryers
1	2½ pound beef roast (chuck, eye of round or tenderloin)
1	1½-2 pound pork roast
2	garlic cloves, chopped
2	large onions, chopped
2	16-ounce cans creamed corn or 4 cups fresh or frozen
1	28-ounce can crushed tomatoes
2	small cans tomato paste
½	cup Worcestershire sauce
2	tablespoons hot red pepper sauce
¼	cup brown sugar, packed
1	cup ketchup
1½	teaspoons chili powder
1½	pounds shelled lima beans or 2 15-ounce cans, optional
1	teaspoon black pepper
¼	cup vinegar
1	teaspoon celery seed

Preheat oven to 375°.

Place fryers in Dutch oven and cover with water. Bring to boil. Reduce heat and simmer 1 hour. Remove fryers and place in bowl to cool. Remove meat and discard bones. Keep broth in Dutch oven.

While fryers are boiling, trim beef and pork roasts and grill or bake in 375° oven in roasting pan until tender, about 1½ hours.

Add garlic, onions, corn, tomatoes, tomato paste, Worcestershire and hot red pepper sauce to Dutch oven with broth. Stir well.

Chop fryer meat and add to broth. Chop beef and pork, or grind in meat grinder and add to broth. Add remaining ingredients. Cover and simmer for 1½ hours. Taste and adjust seasonings.

Makes more than 2 gallons

can do ahead
can freeze

Groundnut Stew

A Ghanian specialty with a memorable sauce

> 1   pound chicken breasts or thighs, bones in
> 1   pound stew beef
>   canola or olive oil for sautéing
> ½   cup chopped onions
> 1   teaspoon salt
> 4   cups water
> 1   large peeled onion
> 2   large tomatoes
> 1   tablespoon tomato puree
> 1   cup natural peanut butter, smooth
> ½   teaspoon white or red hot pepper
>   basil leaves to taste

Sauté chicken and beef with small amount of oil in large, deep pot or Dutch oven. Add chopped onions, salt and 1 cup water. Cover and cook 5 minutes over medium heat.

Uncover and add 3 more cups water, peeled onion, tomatoes and puree. Bring to a boil for 15 minutes.

Remove meat and set aside. Place cooked onion and tomatoes in blender with peanut butter and mix, in batches, if necessary.

Add tomato/peanut butter mixture back into pot with meat. Stir and add salt and pepper to taste.

Bring to boil, reduce heat and simmer uncovered for 45 minutes. Watch that liquid does not boil over.

Serve with steamed rice or boiled potatoes.

Serves 4-6

 can do ahead

> *"Back home in Ghana, folks go to the market to buy fresh nuts they then must roast, peel and grind into paste. But the delicious taste and nutritional value compensate for the long process of cooking."*
>
> *Henrietta Kisseih, Woodward parent*

Cook's Tip:
Be careful not to over-fill your blender with hot food which tends to expand and overflow.

Turkey Sausage Gumbo

The tastiest answer we know for what to do with your turkey carcass the day after the big meal.

1	turkey carcass
12	cups water
4	tablespoons flour
4	tablespoons vegetable oil
1	cup chopped green onions
1	cup chopped celery
4	tablespoons chopped fresh parsley
3	bay leaves
½	teaspoon thyme
2	cups chopped hot, smoked or andouille sausage
4	cups turkey meat from carcass
1	teaspoon salt
½	teaspoon black pepper
1-2	pounds fresh okra or frozen okra slices, to taste
	cooked rice

In large kettle, cover turkey carcass with 12 cups water and boil until meat is easily removed from bones, about 1 hour. Remove carcass and pick meat off bones. Strain and reserve 10 cups turkey broth.

Make roux by browning flour in oil over medium low heat, stirring frequently, until mixture is rich, dark brown, about 10 minutes. Add onions, celery and parsley, then sauté 5 minutes. Slowly add reserved broth to roux. Add bay leaves, thyme, sausage, salt and pepper. Cook over low heat 1½ to 2 hours.

Meanwhile wash and slice fresh okra or thaw frozen. Sauté in a little oil until all ropiness is gone.

Add okra and turkey meat to gumbo ½ hour before completion.

Remove bay leaves and serve gumbo over hot rice.

Serves 8-12

 can do ahead

"Gumbo without okra isn't gumbo. The Creole word for okra is "gumbo." Leave it out to make Turkey Sausage Soup, which is delicious. But don't call it gumbo. You will confuse the children."

Harry McEnerny, Woodward parent

Cook's Tip:

As in all Cajun recipes, proportions and spices are up to the user. If you have more or less turkey meat or sausage, use more or less turkey or sausage and broth, make a bigger or smaller roux, adjust seasoning and use more or less okra.

If you use andouille sausage, leave out the black pepper unless you want it hot. If you want it hotter, add a little cayenne pepper.

Seafood Gumbo Commander's Palace

At the request of his niece, this recipe was faxed to us by Jamie Shannon, the executive chef of the renowned New Orleans restaurant Commander's Palace. We've adapted it slightly for home kitchens.

¾   cup peanut oil
¾   cup flour

2   cups chopped onion
1½   cups chopped green pepper
1   cup chopped celery
¼   cup minced garlic (1 head)
6   cups crab stock with shrimp heads or bottled clam juice
4   bay leaves
1½   pounds peeled shrimp
2   cups fresh okra, sliced
24   fresh oysters with liquid
1   tablespoon filé powder
2½   tablespoons seafood seasoning
1   pound crab meat
1½   ounces hot sauce

In a heavy duty sauce pot, heat oil to smoking point. Add flour slowly, stirring with a wooden spoon. Stir roux constantly until dark brown but not burnt. Roux requires constant stirring and attention.

When roux is dark brown, add onion, peppers, celery and garlic. Stir and cook until onions are clear. Add stock or clam juice and whisk slowly into roux to avoid lumps. Add bay leaves and cook for 20 minutes.

Add shrimp to stock and let cook for 2 minutes. Add okra and stir with wooden spoon. Stir in filé powder and seafood seasoning. Add oysters and bring to boil. Add crab meat, check for seasonings and sprinkle on hot sauce as needed.

Serves 6-10

"I think my uncle Jamie is the greatest cook in the world."

Christi Mallia, first grade Woodward student

Cook's Tip:

Filé powder is the ground leaves of the sassafras tree. It is used to thicken and flavor gumbos and Creole dishes. It should be added to a dish late in the cooking process as it becomes tough and stringy with prolonged heating.

Cioppino

Seafood stew with a San Francisco taste

1	large onion, chopped
1	medium green pepper, halved, seeded and chopped
½	cup sliced celery
1	carrot, pared and shredded
4	garlic cloves, minced
3	tablespoons olive oil
2	1-pound cans whole tomatoes, cut into quarters and drained
1	8-ounce can tomato sauce
1	teaspoon crumbled dried basil
1	bay leaf
	salt and freshly ground black pepper to taste
12	clams, scrubbed and bearded
12	mussels, scrubbed and bearded
1½	cups dry vermouth
1	pound fresh shrimp, shelled and deveined
1	pound fresh scallops
¼	cup minced fresh parsley

In deep pot, sauté onion, green pepper, celery, carrot and garlic in olive oil until softened. Stir in tomatoes, tomato sauce, basil, bay leaf, salt and pepper. Heat to boiling, then lower heat. Cover and simmer 2 hours.

Discard bay leaf. Stir vermouth into sauce. Add shrimp and scallops. Simmer, covered, 10 minutes longer. Place clams and mussels in layer in pot. Cover. Steam 5-10 minutes or until shells are fully opened. Discard any unopened clams or mussels.

Ladle into soup bowls. Sprinkle with fresh parsley to garnish. Serve with sourdough or other crusty bread.

Serves 8

"My mother and I made this stew every year on December 23. Then, after mass on Christmas eve, we'd add the seafood and serve it with Caesar Salad (page 54) and sourdough bread. I continue the tradition with my husband and my daughter Ali."

Kathleen Saurer,
Woodward parent

Cook's Tip:

The beard is the sinew on the shell that attaches the mussel or clam to its resting place in the ocean. To remove the beard, pull off by hand or cut with scissors.

New England Clam Chowder

This is a hearty chowder which may well be considered a main course.

2	potatoes, skinned and diced into ½-inch cubes
2	onions, finely chopped
3	celery stalks, finely chopped
½	cup butter
1	cup flour
2	cups chopped clams, with juice
1	8-ounce bottle clam juice
1	quart half-and-half
8	bacon strips, cooked and finely chopped
½	cup finely chopped parsley
	dash thyme
	seafood seasoning, to taste
	freshly cracked black pepper, to taste

Boil potatoes in water until barely cooked through. Rinse in cold water and set aside.

Sauté onions and celery in butter until vegetables are transparent. Add flour and stir into paste. Cook for 3 minutes over medium heat, stirring constantly. Add clams and juice, then half-and-half, mixing thoroughly after each addition. Bring to boil. Add bacon, parsley, thyme, potatoes and spices. Simmer gently 10 minutes more.

Serve in generous bowls, garnished with chopped fresh parsley. A dark bread like pumpernickel makes a good accompaniment.

Serves 4-6

 easy

Cook's Tip:

The type of potato you use in a dish depends on what you want the potato to do. If you want it to hold its shape, as in the chowder recipe or in a potato salad, choose a red or white round potato; these thin skinned, waxy potatoes have less starch and more moisture than baking potatoes, like russets, which tend to fall apart when boiled. New potatoes are potatoes of any variety that have been dug before they are mature and their sugar has yet to be fully converted to starch; these can be pan roasted or boiled and make great potato salad. Store potatoes in a cool, dark, well ventilated place for up to 2 weeks. New potatoes should be used within 3 days of purchase.

Shrimp and Feta Stew

Serve in large bowls with crusty French bread to sop up the luscious sauce. And be forewarned — there will be requests for seconds.

½ cup minced onion
1½ tablespoons butter
1½ tablespoons oil
½ cup dry white wine
4 ripe tomatoes, peeled, seeded and chopped
1 garlic clove, minced
1 teaspoon salt
¼ teaspoon freshly ground pepper
¾ teaspoon oregano
4 ounces feta cheese, crumbled
1 pound raw shrimp, shelled and deveined

¼ cup chopped fresh parsley

In heavy skillet, sauté onion in butter and oil until soft. Add wine, tomatoes, garlic, salt, pepper and oregano. Bring to boil, lower heat and simmer briefly until sauce is slightly thickened.

Stir in cheese and simmer for 10 to 15 minutes. Adjust seasoning.

Just before serving add shrimp and cook 5 minutes, until shrimp are just tender. Garnish with parsley.

Serves 4

Pasta
and
Rice

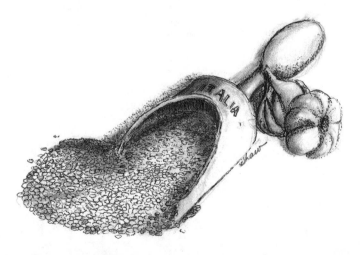

Pasta and Rice

Menu
Hearty Italian Dinner for Six..98

Marinara Sauce Mazzetta

This is the classic sauce, direct from Umbria, Italy.

2	tablespoons extra virgin olive oil
3-5	garlic cloves, finely chopped
1	32-ounce can Italian plum tomatoes
10	fresh basil leaves, broken up, or 2 tablespoons dried basil
1-2	chopped dried hot peppers, to taste

Sauté garlic in olive oil. Add tomatoes and spices. Simmer for at least 30 minutes, stirring.

Serve over pasta or seafood.

Makes about 2 cups

easy
can do ahead

Linguini with Tomatoes, Onions and Capers

¼	cup olive oil
3	garlic cloves, chopped
2	onions, thinly sliced
1	28-ounce can Italian plum tomatoes
2-3	tablespoons capers
½	cup chopped fresh parsley
	salt and pepper to taste
1	pound linguini
	Parmesan cheese to taste

Sauté garlic and onion in oil over low heat for 30 minutes, being careful not to brown.

Drain tomatoes and chop into pieces. Add to onions and cook 15 minutes longer. Add capers and parsley. Season with salt and pepper to taste.

Boil 6 quarts of water and cook linguini until al dente, 3-4 minutes.

Serve sauce over linguini. Pass cheese separately.

Serves 4-6

easy

"When I was a child in Italy we usually had this sauce on pasta on Fridays because we could have no meat. I remember watching the women gathering tomatoes during long evenings in the mountains. They would boil the tomatoes and put them in big jars to use throughout the year."

Tito Mazzetta,
Woodward parent

Variations:
Finely grated carrot, bell peppers and/or celery can be added to marinara sauce during sautéing.

Cook's Tip:
To keep hot pasta hot longer, serve on warmed plates.

Green Lasagna with Walnuts

½ pound whole wheat or green lasagna noodles
2 pounds fresh spinach, well rinsed and stemmed, or
2 10-ounce boxes frozen spinach
2 eggs, lightly beaten
¼ teaspoon freshly grated nutmeg
1 quart tomato sauce or marinara sauce (page 97)
1½ cups coarsely chopped walnuts
1 pound ricotta cheese
1 pound grated or sliced mozzarella cheese
1 cup grated Parmesan or Romano cheese to taste

Preheat oven to 350°.

Cook lasagna noodles according to package directions.

Place fresh spinach in medium skillet with just the water that clings to it after rinsing. Cover pan and cook over medium heat until tender, 3-5 minutes. Drain and press out excess moisture with paper towels. If using frozen spinach, thaw and press to dry. Coarsely chop spinach and mix with eggs and nutmeg.

Layer ingredients in 9x13-inch baking dish in the following order: tomato sauce, lasagna noodles, spinach mixture, walnuts, ricotta cheese, mozzarella, Parmesan or Romano cheese. Repeat layering. End with layer of tomato sauce topped with mozzarella and Parmesan cheese.

Bake lasagna in 350° oven 30-40 minutes (slightly longer if you are using cold tomato sauce) until cheese is melted and casserole is heated through. Then turn oven off and leave lasagna in oven about 30 minutes, or until ready to serve.

Serve with tossed salad of fresh vegetables, hard-cooked eggs and capers in vinaigrette.

Serves 6

can do ahead
can freeze

Pasta with Fresh Tomatoes and Basil

  6   medium ripe tomatoes
  2   tablespoons chopped fresh parsley
10   fresh basil leaves, minced (or 1 teaspoon dried basil)
  ¼ cup lemon juice
  2   tablespoons olive oil
  2   garlic cloves, minced
  1   teaspoon salt
  ½ teaspoon black pepper

Peel and chop tomatoes. Drain for 1 hour. Combine tomatoes with remaining ingredients and refrigerate. Keeps several days in refrigerator.

Serve over any type of cooked pasta, warm or cold.

Serves 4-6

easy
can do ahead

Easy Manicotti with Cheese

  3   cups marinara sauce (page 97), divided
  1   cup water
1¾ cup part skim milk ricotta cheese, no-fat okay
  2   cups shredded mozzarella cheese
  ¼ cup grated Parmesan cheese
  1   egg, slightly beaten
  2   tablespoons chopped fresh parsley
  ½ teaspoon salt
  ¼ teaspoon pepper
  1   8-ounce box manicotti, uncooked

Preheat oven to 400°.

Combine 1½ cups of marinara sauce and ½ cup water and pour into bottom of 13x9x2-inch pan.

In large bowl, stir together cheeses, egg, parsley, salt and pepper. Spoon into uncooked manicotti shells. You will fill about 10 shells. Place shells in pan.

Combine remaining 1½ cups of sauce and ½ cup water and pour over stuffed manicotti. Cover with foil. Bake 40 minutes until hot and bubbly.

Serves 6-8

can do ahead

Cook's Tip:

To save cooked pasta, toss with oil and cover with a damp cloth in the refrigerator. When ready to use, dip in boiling water for 1 to 2 seconds to reheat.

Pasta Provençal

Hearty, vegetarian fare with a Mediterranean flavor

3	tablespoons olive oil
5-6	garlic cloves, peeled and chopped
1-4	1-inch to 2-inch dried red chili peppers, broken into pieces
	freshly ground black pepper
1	pound fresh mushrooms, stemmed and sliced
2	28-ounce cans whole plum tomatoes with puree, cut into pieces
4	sprigs fresh rosemary, leaves stripped from stems and chopped
1	3-ounce can tomato paste
¾	cup sliced black olives, preferably Greek
1	pound dried ziti or penne
	freshly grated Romano cheese

Heat olive oil in large skillet and sauté garlic, red peppers and black pepper until garlic just begins to brown. Add mushrooms and sauté until soft. Add tomatoes with puree, rosemary and tomato paste. Bring to boil, reduce to simmer and cook, uncovered, for 20 minutes. Add olives and heat through.

Meanwhile cook pasta according to package instructions.

Serve sauce over cooked pasta with freshly grated Romano cheese.

Serves 4-6

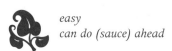
easy
can do (sauce) ahead

Pasta with Sweet Red Pepper Sauce

Unusual and full of zip

5-6	red bell peppers, roasted and peeled (page 21)
3	garlic cloves, peeled
½	cup fresh cilantro
¼	cup fresh lime juice
½	teaspoon ground red/cayenne pepper, or to taste
1	pound pasta, cooked to package directions
	freshly ground Romano cheese

In a food processor or blender, puree roasted peppers, garlic, cilantro, lime juice and cayenne pepper. Serve over cooked pasta and top with grated Romano cheese to taste.

Serves 10

quick and easy
can do ahead
can freeze

Pasta with Light Alfredo Sauce

1	pound cooked pasta
1½	tablespoons melted butter
3	garlic cloves, minced
1½	tablespoons all-purpose flour
2	cups skim milk
3	tablespoons light cream cheese
1-1½	cups Parmesan cheese
	chopped parsley

Sauté garlic in butter. Add flour and stir for 1-2 minutes. Slowly add milk to make a white sauce. Remove from heat. Add cheeses and parsley. Stir until cheeses are well mixed. Toss with hot pasta and serve.

Serves 4-6

quick and easy

Variation:
For a sauce with a little less bite, mix equal parts of red pepper sauce with your favorite marinara sauce. Freeze remaining red pepper sauce for another time.

Variations:
Add your choice of broccoli, asparagus, red or yellow pepper, shrimp or chicken. Be creative with whatever you have on hand.

Pasta with Walnut Pesto Cream

2 cups basil leaves, thoroughly washed and patted dry
4 large garlic cloves, peeled and chopped
1 cup shelled walnuts
1 cup olive oil
1 cup freshly grated imported Parmesan cheese
¼ cup freshly grated imported Romano cheese
salt and freshly ground black pepper to taste

1 pound linguini
¼ cup heavy cream
1 cup pesto
freshly ground black pepper
freshly grated imported Parmesan or Romano cheese

Combine basil, garlic and nuts in bowl of food processor (or halve recipe and use blender) and chop. With motor running, add olive oil in slow, steady stream. Shut off motor, add cheeses, salt and pepper. Process briefly to combine, then scrape out into bowl and cover until ready to use. You will have approximately 2 cups pesto. Pesto can be made ahead and refrigerated for several days or frozen.

Cook linguini according to package instructions. Before draining pasta, remove 2 tablespoons of hot pasta water. Add water to ¼ cup heavy cream and stir into 1 cup pesto.

Drain pasta and return to hot pan. Stir in pesto cream and toss well to combine. Serve immediately on warm plates.

Serves 4-6

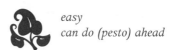

easy
can do (pesto) ahead

Variation:

Using pine nuts in place of walnuts creates a more traditional pesto.

Cook's Tip:

Spread leftover pesto onto cookie sheet and freeze. When pesto is frozen hard, cut it into bars and keep in ziplock bags in freezer until needed in other recipes.

Pasta with Herbs and Garlic

The remarkable thing about pasta dishes is how a few simple ingredients create such complex flavors.

1	1-pound package fettucini
4	tablespoons butter
4	tablespoons olive oil
6	garlic cloves, pressed
4	tablespoons fresh chopped basil
4	tablespoons fresh snipped chives
4	tablespoons fresh chopped parsley
½	cup grated Parmesan cheese
	salt and pepper to taste

Cook and drain pasta.

Meanwhile, in sauce pan, melt butter over low heat. Add oil. Press garlic into butter and oil. Cook 3-5 minutes, until lightly browned.

Pour garlic mixture over hot pasta and toss well. Add herbs and cheese. Salt and pepper to taste.

Toss and serve immediately.

Serves 4-6

 *quick and easy*

Cook's Tip:

Extra virgin olive oil refers to the first cold pressing of the olive. The best tasting and most expensive olive oil, it should be used when the oil's flavor is dominant, as in garlic bread. You can use less expensive virgin olive oils for sautéing. The flavors of olive oils can vary greatly. It is best to try a variety of oils until you hit on one you like. The oils from Spain and Italy are particularly nice. There are also many good olive oils coming out of California now. Olive oil should be stored in a cool, dark place to protect its flavor.

Italian Garlic Bread

This is the classic Italian version.

1 large loaf French or Italian bread
6 garlic cloves
½ cup extra virgin olive oil
  salt and freshly ground pepper

Cut bread into 1-inch slices. Place on hot grill or under broiler and toast on both sides. Peel and crush garlic slightly. Rub grilled bread on both sides with crushed garlic. Brush generously with olive oil and sprinkle with salt and freshly ground pepper.

Ziti with Ricotta and Sausage

1 pound fresh Italian sausage, half hot, half mild
2 tablespoons olive oil
1 large onion, chopped
6 garlic cloves, minced
2 28-ounce cans Italian tomatoes, with juice
1 tablespoon dried basil or ¼ cup chopped fresh
1 teaspoon fennel seed
  salt and pepper to taste
1 pound ziti
1 cup ricotta
¼ cup Parmesan cheese
¼ cup fresh chopped basil

Remove sausage from its casing, crumble and brown. Drain well, remove from skillet, and wipe out excess fat. Add 2 tablespoons olive oil to skillet. Add onions and garlic, then cook until onions are soft.

Puree tomatoes in blender or food processor. Add to skillet along with basil, fennel seed, salt and pepper. Return sausage to pan and allow to simmer, uncovered, about 30 minutes.

Cook pasta according to package directions, drain and return to pot. Add 2 cups of sauce and toss with pasta. Add ricotta, Parmesan and basil. Stir to combine.

Top each serving with extra sauce and Parmesan cheese.

Serves 4-6 with sauce left over

Ziti with Tomato and Smoked Mozzarella

1 pound ziti
1-2 tablespoons olive oil
1 small yellow onion, coarsely chopped
1 large garlic clove, minced
1 28-ounce can crushed tomatoes in tomato puree
1 teaspoon sugar
¾ teaspoon salt
¼ teaspoon dried hot red pepper flakes
¼ cup packed fresh basil leaves
8 ounces smoked mozzarella cheese
2 tablespoons balsamic vinegar

grated Parmesan cheese

Cook pasta according to package directions.

While pasta cooks, heat oil in large saucepan over medium heat and cook onion and garlic 2 minutes. Add tomatoes, sugar, salt and pepper flakes and bring to a boil. Reduce heat and simmer, uncovered, 5 minutes.

While tomatoes are cooking, cut basil into thin strips. Cut cheese into ½ to ¾ inch strips or grate. Set aside.

Drain pasta, add to tomato sauce and toss lightly. Add vinegar, basil, and cheese. Toss again. Sprinkle with Parmesan cheese.

Serve with mixed green salad and garlic bread.

Serves 4

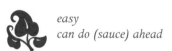

easy
can do (sauce) ahead

Southern Garlic Bread

This Americanized version is also delicious.

1 large garlic clove
½ cup butter, softened
3 tablespoons fresh herbs or 1 tablespoon dried, optional large loaf French or Italian bread

Crush garlic to paste, then add to softened butter with herbs, if desired. Possible herbs to use include chives, basil, tarragon, parsley or thyme, or some combination. Mix well. Can be done ahead of time and refrigerated; return to room temperature before using.

Cut bread into 1-inch slices going to within ½-inch of loaf bottom. Spread butter between slices. Wrap in aluminum foil and place in 350° oven for 10-15 minutes or until top is crisp. Or place on grill and cook about 5 minutes per side.

Penne with Broccoli and Parmesan

3	tablespoons olive oil
2-3	garlic cloves, minced
1-2	dry hot peppers (pepperoncini), finely chopped or 4 roasted peppers from a jar
8	broccoli crowns
¼	teaspoon salt
1	pound penne, or pasta of choice
	freshly ground Parmesan cheese
	freshly ground black pepper

"This recipe was first prepared by a dear friend and talented chef from Rome, Italy, while he was our guest."

Amy Mazzetta, Woodward parent

In large skillet, sauté garlic in olive oil. Add dried hot peppers. Set aside.

Bring large pot of salted water to boil, add broccoli and cook until tender. Remove broccoli but DO NOT drain water. Add pasta to water and boil 6-7 minutes until very al dente.

Chop broccoli fine and add to garlic/pepper mixture. Heat through.

Drain pasta and add to broccoli. Continue to cook in pan 1-2 minutes longer.

Toss with Parmesan and black pepper and serve.

Serves 4 (8 as side dish)

Variations:
Red and yellow bell peppers can be used in place of broccoli. Mushrooms can be added with the broccoli.

 easy

Thai Shrimp and Sesame Noodles

*The combination of sesame and peanut gives this dish a wonderful,
almost smoky flavor.*

1	pound shrimp, shelled and deveined
1	cup vinaigrette (page 54)
2	tablespoons chunky peanut butter
1	tablespoon soy sauce
1	tablespoon honey
1	tablespoon peeled and grated fresh ginger
½	teaspoon crushed red pepper
1	8-ounce package angel hair pasta
2	tablespoons vegetable oil
1	tablespoon sesame oil
1	carrot, peeled and shredded
1	cup chopped green onion
¼	cup chopped cilantro

About 1¼ hours before serving combine shrimp and ⅓ cup dressing.
Cover and refrigerate.

With whisk or fork, mix peanut butter, soy sauce, honey, ginger, red
pepper and remaining dressing. Set aside.

After shrimp have marinated 1 hour, prepare pasta according to
package directions. Drain.

In large skillet over high heat, heat vegetable and sesame oils until hot.
Add carrot and cook 1 minute.

Drain dressing off shrimp. Add shrimp and green onion to carrot and
cook about 3 minutes, stirring constantly, until shrimp turn pink.

Toss pasta with peanut butter mixture and shrimp mixture. Sprinkle
with cilantro.

Serves 4

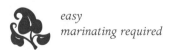
*easy
marinating required*

Cook's Tip:

*Sesame oil comes in
two varieties. The one
called for in recipes in
this book is the dark,
strongly flavored
sesame oil made from
toasted sesame seeds.
It is widely used in
Asian and Indian
dishes and imparts a
wonderful nutty
flavor to dishes that
no other ingredient
can duplicate. The
other type of sesame
oil is cold pressed
from untoasted seeds.
Light in color with a
mild flavor, it is best
in salad dressings or
for sautéing.*

Linguini with Blackened Scallops

Variation:

*You can substitute
shrimp for scallops.
Peel and devein
shrimp before using.
Cook shrimp until just
pink, about 2 minutes,
before removing
from skillet.*

2   pounds raw scallops
4   tablespoons blackened redfish seasoning
5   tablespoons olive oil, divided
1   pound fresh mushrooms, stemmed, washed and sliced
2   shallots, chopped
1¼ cups dry white wine
1   cup sour cream
2   tablespoons cornstarch
2   cups chicken broth
1   12-ounce jar roasted red peppers, drained and sliced
    into strips
1   pound linguini

Mix blackened seasoning and 3 tablespoons of oil in bowl and add
scallops. Toss to coat evenly and set aside.

In heavy skillet heat 2 remaining tablespoons of oil and sauté
mushrooms and shallots until tender. Add scallops and cook 1 minute,
or until scallops are cooked through. Remove scallops. Add wine to
mushroom mixture in skillet and bring to boil. Boil several minutes.

Meanwhile, mix sour cream and cornstarch together in small bowl.
Add chicken broth and stir to mix. Add to mushrooms in skillet and
stir. Cook until bubbly and thickened. Add scallops and peppers and
heat through.

Serve over hot cooked linguini.

Serves 4-6

Caribbean Rice and Beans

1½ teaspoons olive oil
  1 large roasted red bell pepper (page 21) or ½ cup rinsed
     peppers from a jar, cut in strips
  ½ green bell pepper, cut in strips
  2 garlic cloves, finely chopped
  2 16-ounce cans black beans, drained and rinsed
  2 15-ounce cans chopped tomatoes, drained
  2 tablespoons vinegar, preferably white distilled
  5 dashes hot red pepper sauce, or to taste
  3 cups cooked rice (1 cup raw)
  3 tablespoons finely chopped fresh cilantro
     salt and freshly ground pepper to taste

In a large pan, heat oil over medium heat until hot but not smoking.
Add red and green peppers and garlic. Sauté 2 minutes.

Add black beans, tomatoes, vinegar and hot red pepper sauce. Bring to
a boil, then reduce heat to low. Cover and simmer 5 minutes. Stir in
cooked rice and cilantro. Adjust seasonings.

Serves 6

 *easy*
do ahead

Variation:
*You can add 3 cups of
cooked, chopped
turkey or chicken.*

Spring Vegetable Risotto

3   cups chicken stock
3   tablespoons butter
1   medium onion, finely chopped
1   cup arborio rice
¼   cup dry white wine
¼   teaspoon saffron threads or ¼ teaspoon turmeric
2   cups chopped blanched vegetables, (asparagus, zucchini, yellow squash, bell peppers, peas, scallions)
¼   cup freshly grated Parmesan cheese
    salt and pepper to taste

In sauce pan bring chicken stock to boil, lower heat and simmer gently until ready to use in recipe.

In heavy saucepan, melt 1½ tablespoons butter over moderate heat. Sauté onion until softened but not brown.

Mix in rice, tossing 1-2 minutes to coat grains. Add wine and saffron threads. Cook until liquid is almost absorbed, stirring frequently.

Pour in 1 cup chicken stock and simmer until rice is nearly dry, stirring frequently. Repeat with second cup of stock. Repeat with rest of stock. Add vegetables and heat entire mixture through.

Remove from stove. Combine with remaining 1½ tablespoons butter and Parmesan cheese. Season with salt and pepper and serve.

Serves 4

Saffron and Red Pepper Rice

This will spice up a no-frills beef tenderloin or cool down a spicy hot curry.

- 3 cups chicken broth
- 2 tablespoons butter
- 1 teaspoon salt
- ¼ teaspoon ground turmeric
- ⅛ teaspoon ground saffron
- 2 cups uncooked long grain rice, preferably basmati
- 1 10-ounce package frozen English peas
- 1 cup diced sweet red pepper
- ¼ cup chopped green onions

Combine first 5 ingredients in large, heavy saucepan and bring to boil. Gradually add rice, stirring constantly. Cover, reduce heat and simmer 10 minutes. Stir in English peas, red pepper and green onions. Cover and simmer 10 minutes more or until rice is tender.

Serves 12

 easy

Five Spice Rice

- 1 tablespoon vegetable oil
- 1 garlic clove, crushed
- 1 teaspoon minced fresh ginger
- ¼ cup minced green onion
- 2 teaspoons five spice powder
- 1 cup rice
- 2 cups chicken stock or water
  salt to taste

Heat oil in large sauce pan. Add garlic, ginger and green onion. Sauté about five minutes. Add five spice powder and rice, then stir to coat rice with oil. Add stock or water and bring to simmer. If using unsalted stock, add salt to taste. Reduce heat and cover. Cook 20 minutes or until all liquid is absorbed.

Serves 4

 easy

Cook's Tip:
Five spice powder is a spice mixture consisting of equal amounts of cinnamon, cloves, fennel seed, star anise and Szechuan peppercorns. It is used extensively in Chinese cooking and can be found in either the spice or the international food section of most grocery stores.

Basmati Rice with Golden Raisins and Almonds

With its slightly sweet flavor, this is an excellent accompaniment for spicy stews.

2	tablespoons olive oil
1	garlic clove, crushed
2½	teaspoons ground cumin
1	teaspoon ground coriander
2	cups basmati rice
4	cups chicken stock or water
½	cup golden raisins
½	cup slivered almonds, toasted in 350° oven until golden, 5-7 minutes
	salt and pepper to taste

In saucepan, heat olive oil. Briefly sauté garlic, then add cumin and coriander. Add rice and stir to coat. Add chicken stock or water, bring to a boil, stir, then lower heat and cook 17-20 minutes until all liquid is absorbed.

Fluff with fork and add raisins and almonds. Check seasonings and add salt and pepper as needed.

Serves 6-8

 easy

Noodle Kugel

This sweet side dish is traditionally served on Jewish holidays alongside a brisket of beef or roasted chicken. Every family has its own favorite variation.

½	pound noodles
¼	cup slivered almonds
¼	cup dried chopped apricots, cherries or cranberries
¼	cup raisins
1	cup sour cream
2	cups milk
3	large eggs or 1 egg and 2 egg whites
⅓	cup melted butter
2	cups cottage cheese
½	cup plus 2 tablespoons sugar
2	teaspoons cinnamon

Preheat oven to 350°.

Cook noodles according to package directions. Drain. Combine next 8 ingredients and mix with noodles. Pour into greased 9x12-inch casserole dish.

Mix together sugar and cinnamon and sprinkle over kugel. Bake in 350° oven for 45 minutes. This will keep refrigerated for a couple of days or can be frozen. Heat through before serving.

Serve instead of mashed potatoes as an accompaniment to beef brisket and steamed vegetables.

Serves 10-12

*easy
can do ahead*

Rice and Noodle Pilaf

2 teaspoons vegetable oil
¾ cup spaghetti broken into 1-inch pieces
3 tablespoons minced green onion
¾ cup rice
2 cups chicken stock
2 tablespoons minced fresh flat leaf parsley
  salt and pepper to taste

In heavy saucepan, heat oil, add spaghetti and stir until golden brown. Add green onion and rice and cook for a few minutes more. Add stock and bring to boil. Reduce heat to low and simmer until all liquid is absorbed, about 20 minutes.

Remove from heat and fluff with fork. Add parsley, salt and pepper and serve.

Serves 4

*quick and easy
can do ahead*

Meat and Game

Meat and Game

Rolled Flank Steak in Gingered Broth

Perfect for entertaining because it is so easy yet elegant

¼	cup butter
½	cup chopped onion
1	garlic clove, crushed
1½	cups cooked rice
½	cup chopped fresh parsley
½	cup Parmesan cheese
½	teaspoon salt
¼	teaspoon pepper

1¾-2	pounds flank steak
1	garlic clove
2	tablespoons soy sauce
½	teaspoon pepper
2	tablespoons butter
1	cup beef broth
½	cup water
1	tablespoon grated fresh ginger

Preheat oven to 350°.

To make filling, sauté onion and garlic in butter until onions are golden. Remove from heat. Stir in cooked rice, parsley, cheese, salt and pepper.

Score steak lightly on both sides. Rub both sides with garlic, brush with soy sauce and sprinkle with pepper. Lay steak flat and spread with 1 tablespoon butter. Place rice stuffing over steak about 1-2 inches from edges. Roll up steak from end to end. Fasten and secure with tooth picks. Spread remaining butter over steak.

Pour beef broth over steak roll. Sprinkle with ginger. Bake at 350° 45-60 minutes depending on how you prefer your meat done.

Serves 4

 *easy*
can do ahead

Menu

Classic
Dinner
Party

French Pâtè
Battistini
34

Eggless Caesar
Salad
54

Rolled Flank Steak
in Gingered Broth
117

Sautéed Kale
165

Rosemary Potatoes
177
or
New Potatoes
Bavarian Style
176

Apple Custard
Tart in
Shortbread Crust
191

Shredded Beef with Green Pepper

Cook's Tip:
Partially frozen meat cuts more easily than fully thawed.

1 pound flank steak or London broil
2 tablespoons soy sauce
1 tablespoon cold water
2 teaspoons cornstarch
½ teaspoon salt
1 tablespoon cooking oil
½ tablespoon red wine, optional
1 green onion, cut in 1-inch lengths
3 ¼-inch slices fresh ginger
2 green peppers, halved and seeds removed
½ teaspoon sugar
1 tablespoon soy sauce
  oil for sautéing

Slice beef very thin at an angle against the grain. Mix next six ingredients and marinate beef for 1 hour.

Thinly slice onion, ginger and peppers. Set each aside.

In large pan, sauté beef in small amount of oil until almost cooked, about 10 seconds. Remove beef and set aside.

Add 1 tablespoon oil to pan and stir fry ginger and onion. Add green peppers, salt and sugar. Continue frying about 5 minutes. Peppers should remain green and somewhat crunchy.

Add beef and mix into vegetables, cooking another minute or so.

Serve with rice and pan sautéed sugar snap peas.

Serves 4

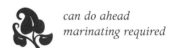

*can do ahead
marinating required*

Kousa Mahshi

The lemon juice and mint combine beautifully in this Middle Eastern dish of stuffed squash in tomato sauce.

8	medium to large yellow squash
1	pound ground beef
1	cup medium grain rice
1	teaspoon cumin
1	teaspoon saffron or paprika
1	teaspoon salt
¼	teaspoon black pepper, or more to taste
1	cup tomato sauce
4	cups water
5	garlic cloves, crushed into paste with 1 teaspoon salt
1	tablespoon powdered dried mint
	juice of 1 lemon or to taste

Cut long necks off squash. Using a peeler, scoop out pulp, being careful not to break skin.

To prepare stuffing, mix beef, rice and spices by hand. Add salt and pepper to taste.

Stuff each squash loosely allowing for rice expansion.

In large sauce pan, combine tomato sauce with water and garlic paste. Bring to boil over medium-high heat. Slowly place stuffed squash in boiling water. Bring back to boil, then reduce heat, cover partially, and let cook 1-1½ hours . Do not let liquids evaporate quickly. There should be plenty of sauce. Add mint and lemon juice near end of cooking time. Check doneness by inserting a fork in one of the squashes.

Serves 4

Variations:
This stuffing also works for stuffed cabbage or stuffed green peppers.

Manny Pink's Brisket

A very traditional Jewish dish that, with its mix of white and sweet potatoes, should be right at home in southern kitchens.

> "My great grand-mother used to make this for the Jewish sabbath while living in Tarnapol, Poland. It was made because it could be put in the oven and left alone while other prepara-tions for the sabbath were being done."
>
> *Dede Leff,*
> *Woodward parent*

1	5-pound brisket, can be slightly bigger or smaller
5	large white potatoes
3	large sweet potatoes
2	pounds carrots
2	large onions, peeled and sliced
1	16-ounce can stewed tomatoes with liquid
3	tablespoons ketchup
	garlic powder to taste

Preheat oven to 250-275°.

Place brisket in large roasting pan.

Peel and slice potatoes and onions. Peel carrots. Grate a few carrots over brisket. Slice the rest. Sprinkle garlic powder over brisket. Surround brisket with vegetables. Spread tomatoes and ketchup over brisket and vegetables. Add about 1 cup water. Cover with foil and roast in 250-275° oven until vegetables are tender, 3-4 hours.

Remove meat from pan to slice, then return to pan and cook another hour.

You can serve immediately or keep refrigerated. It is actually better the next day.

Serves 8

easy
can do ahead
can refrigerate

Meat Loaf Wellington

1   pound lean ground beef
½   cup old fashioned rolled oats
¼   cup chopped celery
¼   cup chopped onion
¼   cup peeled, coarsely grated carrot
¼   cup chopped fresh parsley
1   large egg, lightly beaten
⅓   cup ketchup
½   teaspoon salt
¼   teaspoon black pepper
¼   teaspoon dried oregano
1⅓ cups flour
½   teaspoon salt
½   cup vegetable shortening
3-4 tablespoons cold water
1   egg yolk mixed with 1 tablespoon water

Preheat oven to 450°.

In large bowl, combine beef and next 10 ingredients. Mix well. Cover and refrigerate while making pastry.

In medium bowl, mix flour and salt. Add shortening. Using 2 knives or pastry blender, cut shortening into flour until mixture resembles coarse cornmeal. Sprinkle with 3 tablespoons water and mix with fork until mixture clings together in ball. Add remaining water, if needed. Press dough together with hands.

On floured surface, roll out dough to 14-inch circle. Shape meat into 6-inch ball, flatten slightly and place in center of pastry. Bring edges of pastry above meat and pinch together to enclose completely. Cut off excess pastry. Put pastry-covered loaf, seam side down, in center of ungreased large, low-sided baking pan. Cut small hole on top of loaf for steam to escape. Brush pastry with egg yolk/water mixture.

Press pastry trimmings into ball and roll out ⅛-inch thick. Cut into rounds with 1-inch cutter. Arrange pastry rounds in overlapping circles on top of enclosed meat loaf. Brush with egg yolk mixture.

Bake 10 minutes at 450°, then reduce heat to 350°. Bake 40-50 minutes longer, until lightly browned.

Serves 4-6

"No Fail" Roast

1   3-pound eye of round roast
    salt to taste
    lemon pepper
    garlic powder to taste

Preheat oven to 500°.

Sprinkle salt, pepper and garlic on roast. Place on rack in shallow pan. Cook uncovered 4 minutes per pound for rare, 5 minutes per pound for medium, or 6 minutes per pound for well done.

Turn off oven at end of cooking time but do NOT open oven door for 2 hours.

Slice and serve accompanied by Rosemary Potatoes (page 177) and Bourbon Mushrooms (page 168).

Serves 6-8

 easy

Grilled Lamb with Rosemary and Mint

A simple combination yields a complex flavor.

8   loin lamb chops (2½ pounds), bones in
1   cup mint jelly, divided
2   tablespoons crushed dried rosemary
    salt to taste

In small saucepan, heat ⅔ cup jelly over medium heat to liquify. Stir in rosemary.

Remove jelly mixture from heat and brush over lamb chops. Marinate at least 2 hours in cool room or refrigerator.

Grill chops 7-10 minutes per side according to preferred doneness.

Just before serving, brush remaining ⅓ cup mint jelly over chops. Salt to taste.

Serves 4

 *easy*
marinating required

Armenian Shish Kebab

½ cup olive oil
¼ cup lemon juice
1 teaspoon salt
1 teaspoon dried marjoram
1 teaspoon dried thyme
½ teaspoon freshly ground pepper
1 garlic clove, minced
¼ cup diced onion
2 teaspoons minced fresh parsley
2 pounds boneless leg of lamb, cut into 1½-inch cubes
16 mushroom caps
4 tomatoes, quartered, or 16 salad tomatoes
2 green, yellow, or red peppers, cut in 1-inch squares
2 Spanish onions, cut into eighths (boiled a few minutes until tender)

Combine oil, lemon juice, salt, marjoram, thyme, pepper, garlic, diced onion and parsley for marinade. Pour marinade over lamb cubes, cover and refrigerate 6 hours or longer.

Remove lamb from marinade and drain on paper towels.

Spear lamb cubes, mushroom caps, tomatoes, pepper squares and onions alternately on skewers. Grill, turning occasionally, until cooked to desired doneness, or use individual kebab grilling baskets.

Makes 16 skewers

 *easy*
marinating required

Variations:
These kebabs can also be cooked under the broiler in the oven. The marinade also works on beef chunks.

Cook's Tip:
If using bamboo skewers, soak them in water 20-30 minutes to prevent them from burning on the grill. It is also a good idea to use 2 skewers per kabob to keep the food from swiveling and falling off and to help make turning the kebab easier.

Variation:

Lamb shoulder, a less expensive cut, will also work fine in this recipe.

Lamb Chops with Herbs and Mushrooms

6	boneless loin lamb chops, cut 1 ½-inches thick (about 6 ounces each, trimmed weight)
	salt and freshly ground black pepper to taste
1	tablespoon minced garlic
⅓	cup minced fresh mint and parsley, mixed to taste
2-4	tablespoons sweet butter, room temperature, divided
6	thin lemon slices
2-3	dozen firm white mushroom caps (about 1 pound)

Preheat oven to 350°.

Season lamb chops with salt and pepper to taste.

Mash garlic, herbs and half of butter together into rough paste. Divide mixture among lamb chops, spreading a bit inside tails and the rest on top. Roll up chops into tidy rounds and tie with kitchen twine.

Arrange each chop on piece of aluminum foil and place lemon slice and mint sprig on top of each. Smear remaining butter over mushrooms and arrange them evenly around chops. Season to taste with salt and pepper. Seal foil packets and set on baking sheet. Bake at 350° for about 30 minutes for medium rare.

Transfer packets to serving plates and allow guests to open them at table. Serve with chilled asparagus topped with vinaigrette.

Serves 6

 easy

Lamb in Goan Cashew Cream Sauce

½ teaspoon salt
6 tablespoons freshly ground pepper
½ cup yogurt
½ teaspoon cardamom powder
2 pounds leg of lamb, cut into 1-inch cutlets

1 cup milk
1 cup cashew nuts
¼ cup yogurt
¼ teaspoon salt
   pinch of fresh pepper
4 tablespoons heavy cream

Preheat oven to 400˚.

Mix together first 4 ingredients to make marinade.

Score lamb cutlets lightly in x patterns with knife. Rub in marinade and let lamb marinate 1 hour.

Place lamb on baking sheet and bake 20 minutes. Turn oven off and leave lamb in cooling oven for 10 more minutes.

Meanwhile make sauce. Put milk and cashews in blender and blend to make thin paste. Put paste into small saucepan. Add remaining sauce ingredients. Mix well and bring to boil. Lower heat and simmer 5 minutes.

Add simmering sauce to meat and pan juices. Bake until boiling, then serve immediately, accompanied by rice and green vegetable.

Serves 4

 *marinating requied*

Cold Marinated Pork Loin

Cook's Tip:

If using the marinade to baste the meat, do not baste during the last 10-15 minutes of cooking so that marinade can get hot enough to destroy any dangerous organisms. If marinade is to be used later as part of a sauce, it should be brought to a boil and cooked 2-3 minutes before serving.

Variation:

You can butterfly the loin and roll it around dried prunes and apricots before baking.

1   4-6 pound boneless pork loin roast, rubbed generously with thyme and dry mustard
½   cup dry sherry
½   cup soy sauce
2   tablespoons ground ginger
3   garlic cloves, minced

8   ounces currant, apple or apricot jelly
1   tablespoon soy sauce
2   tablespoons dry sherry

   orange slices

Combine ½ cup sherry, ½ cup soy sauce, ginger and garlic and pour over roast. Marinate several hours or overnight, turning occasionally.

After marinating is complete, preheat oven to 325°.

Remove meat from marinade and reserve marinade. Place pork in roasting pan and bake at 325° for 25 minutes per pound or until meat thermometer reaches 175°, basting often with marinade. Do not baste during last 30 minutes of cooking since marinade was exposed to raw meat.

To prepare glaze, melt jelly over medium heat. Add soy sauce and sherry, mixing well. Cool.

Place roast on a rack in a shallow pan and slice. Spoon glaze over roast. As mixture runs off into pan, repeat to build up a coating.

Serve cold, garnished with orange slices. Also good hot.

Serves 10-12

easy
marinating required

Cranberry Barbeque Pork Roast

4 cups fresh cranberries
1 cup sugar
½ cup Georgia BBQ sauce
½ cup orange juice
1 4-6 pound pork loin roast, bone in

Preheat oven to 450°.

Combine cranberries, sugar, barbeque sauce and orange juice in a large sauce pan, mixing well. Bring to boil over medium heat stirring constantly. Continue to boil 5 minutes. Remove from heat.

Place roast on a rack in a shallow roasting pan, fat side up. Reduce heat at once to 325° and cook uncovered 25 to 35 minutes per pound, or until an internal temperature of about 175° is reached.

Baste roast with sauce during last 30 minutes of baking. Serve with remaining sauce.

Serves 8

 easy

Cook's Tip:
For easier carving, have your butcher cut through the ribs of the roast at their base.

Georgia BBQ Sauce

1 cup ketchup
1 tablespoon Worcestershire sauce
3 dashes hot pepper sauce
1 cup water
¼ cup apple cider vinegar
2 tablespoons sugar
1 teaspoon salt
1 teaspoon celery seed
3 tablespoons spicy brown mustard, optional

Mix ingredients together and simmer for 30 minutes. Serve with pork, beef or chicken.

Pickin' Pork

*This dish gets its name because the meat is fall-apart tender and can
easily be "picked" from the bone.*

1	10 to 12-pound whole or half fresh ham
¼	cup red wine or apple cider vinegar
1	cup finely chopped onion
6	gloves garlic, finely chopped
¼	cup finely chopped fresh sage or 2 tablespoons dried
2	tablespoons freshly ground black pepper
	BBQ sauce
	Dijon mustard
	mayonnaise
	yeast rolls

Preheat oven to 200°.

Remove all visible fat and rind from ham. Rub vinegar, onion, garlic
and sage over entire ham. Press black pepper onto all surfaces. Wrap
very tightly in heavy duty aluminum foil. Seal well so no juices escape.
Refrigerate for 2-4 hours to marinate.

Bake wrapped ham in shallow pan in 200° oven at least 14 hours. This
can be done overnight.

Place on big platter with bowls of BBQ sauce, mustard, mayonnaise,
and yeast rolls.

Serves a crowd

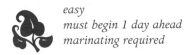

*easy
must begin 1 day ahead
marinating required*

Pork Marabella

1   6-pound boneless pork loin
1   head of garlic, peeled and pureed
1½ tablespoons dried oregano
½   cup red wine vinegar
¼   cup olive oil
1   cup brown sugar
1   cup red wine
½   cup capers with juice
½   cup whole green olives
6   bay leaves
1   cup pitted prunes
1   cup dried apricots
¼   cup fresh parsley or cilantro
    cooked rice

Preheat oven to 350°.

In large bowl, combine garlic, oregano, vinegar, oil, sugar, red wine and caper juice. Pour over pork. Add olives, capers, bay leaves, prunes and apricots. Marinate over night.

Place pork with all marinating ingredients in roasting pan and bake in 350° oven, uncovered, for 1½ hours. Slice meat and sprinkle with parsley or cilantro.

On large platter, arrange meat and cooked fruits surrounded by rice. Degrease pan drippings and serve as sauce.

Serves 10-12

 *marinating required*

Variation:
In place of pork, try 6 pounds of chicken cut into serving pieces.

Spicy Thai Grilled Pork

3   tablespoons olive oil
4   garlic cloves, thinly sliced
2   tablespoons hot Chinese chili oil
2   whole pork tenderloins (about 2 pounds)

6   tablespoons soy sauce
3   tablespoons honey
2-3 tablespoons orange juice
2   tablespoons Chinese sesame oil
2   tablespoons hot Chinese chili oil
1   tablespoon peanut butter
1   teaspoon dried red pepper flakes
2   teaspoons cornstarch dissolved in 1 tablespoon water

Stir olive oil, garlic and hot chili oil together. Roll tenderloins in oil mixture to coat. Refrigerate at least 30 minutes, rotating tenderloins occasionally.

Combine remaining ingredients except cornstarch mixture and heat through, then set aside until ready to proceed.

20 minutes prior to serving, remove tenderloins from marinade and discard marinade. Broil or grill tenderloins for 10-15 minutes, turning once or twice. Carve into ½-inch thick slices.

Reheat sauce and thicken with cornstarch mixture over medium heat, stirring constantly. Pour over tenderloin slices.

Serves 4-6

*easy
can partially do ahead
marinating required*

Taiwanese Sweet and Sour Pork

1   1-pound pork tenderloin

½   tablespoon soy sauce
1   tablespoon corn starch
1   tablespoon cold water
1   egg yolk

3   tablespoons vinegar
4   tablespoons sugar
4   tablespoons ketchup
5   tablespoons cold water
3   teaspoons corn starch
1   teaspoon salt
1   teaspoon sesame oil

½   cup corn starch to coat pork
    peanut oil for frying pork
2   green peppers, cut into 1-inch pieces
6   pineapple slices, cut into 1-inch pieces

Pound pork with back of cleaver to tenderize, then cut into 1-inch cubes. Mix together next 4 ingredients and marinate pork at least ½ hour.

In small bowl, mix together next 7 seasoning sauce ingredients and set aside.

Heat peanut oil in large frying pan to depth of 1 inch. While oil is heating, coat pork pieces in ½ cup cornstarch. Cook pork in oil until brown and cooked through. Remove pork, reheat oil and cook pork again until crispy.

Remove pork and drain oil from pan. Add back 2 tablespoons oil and stir fry green pepper and pineapple, stirring constantly. Add seasoning sauce and continue to stir fry until thickened. Turn off heat, add pork, mix well, and serve immediately with steamed rice.

Serves 4

 *marinating required*

Game Birds with Tarragon Marinade

1	cup olive oil
¼	cup raspberry vinegar
2	tablespoons lemon juice
3	tablespoons chopped fresh tarragon
	black pepper to taste
8	skinless pheasant breasts or equivalent amount of quail, grouse or dove
¼	cup melted butter

In medium to large bowl, mix oil, vinegar, lemon juice and tarragon together and season with pepper. Add game birds to marinade and refrigerate overnight, turning frequently.

Grill game bird, basting frequently with marinade and melted butter.

Serves 8

*quick and easy
marinating required*

Braised Quail

Quail and game birds are often available at specialty food and farmers' markets.

6-8	slices bacon, diced
16	small quail
	salt and pepper to taste
1	cup all-purpose flour
1	cup chopped onion
½	cup finely chopped fresh garlic
1	cup sliced mushrooms
1	cup dry red wine
1	cup beef stock or broth
2	tablespoons tomato paste
1	cup half-and-half, optional

Brown bacon in large, deep pan until crisp. Transfer bacon to towel to drain and pour off some of bacon grease, leaving some in pan.

Season quail with salt and pepper. Dredge lightly in flour. Brown quail in bacon grease over moderately high heat, 2-3 minutes per side.

Transfer quail to warm platter as they brown. Lower heat and add onions, garlic and mushrooms. Cook until onions are transparent, then add wine, beef broth and tomato paste. Return quail to pan, cover and simmer about 30 minutes. Add half-and-half, if desired, and bacon bits. Heat through thoroughly and serve with steamed vegetables, rice pilaf and white wine.

Serves 2-3, depending on quail size

Venison Pot Roast Hungarian Style

1 5-pound venison roast
    several slices bacon or salt pork, cut in 1-inch pieces
2 garlic cloves, slivered
    salt and pepper to taste
    flour
3 tablespoons olive oil
2 onions, coarsely chopped
1 cup beef bouillon
1 cup white wine
3-4 carrots, cut in chunks
3 stalks celery, cut diagonally into chunks
½ teaspoon dried oregano
1 tablespoon minced fresh parsley
1 tablespoon paprika
1 cup sour cream

Cut slits in roast and insert bacon and garlic. Rub roast with salt and pepper, roll in flour to coat.

Heat olive oil in Dutch oven. Sear roast in hot oil until well browned. Add onions, bouillon and wine. Cover and simmer 1½ hours.

Add carrots, celery, oregano, parsley and paprika. Add more bouillon if necessary. Simmer an additional 30 minutes or until meat and vegetables are tender.

Remove to hot platter, reduce liquid if necessary. Add sour cream and heat. Do not boil.

Slice venison and serve with sauce, cooked vegetables and rice.

Serves 8-10

 easy

Venison Scallopine

Hours of simmering create a wonderfully tender dish for game lovers.

Cook's Tip:
To cook in a crock pot, sauté butter, onions, garlic and venison in skillet. Then transfer to crock pot. Cook on high 1 hour, then on low for 8 hours.

2   medium onions, sliced
3   garlic cloves, minced
¼   cup butter
2   pounds thinly sliced venison steak
8   ounces sliced fresh mushrooms
¼   teaspoon pepper
2   teaspoons paprika
⅓   cup chopped fresh parsley
1¼ cups beef bouillon
1½ cups sour cream, light okay
4   tablespoons flour
1   16-ounce package wide noodles

In large Dutch oven, sauté onions and garlic in butter until soft. Add venison and brown on all sides. Add mushrooms and sauté. Add pepper, paprika, parsley and bouillon. Stir all ingredients well.

Reduce heat and simmer, partially covered, six hours. Stir occasionally.

Just before serving, cook noodles according to package directions. Thoroughly mix flour with sour cream, then add to meat, stirring well after each addition. Do not let boil once sour cream is added.

Serve venison over hot, cooked noodles.

Serves 8

 can do ahead

Poultry and Seafood

Poultry and Seafood

Mustard Soy Chicken

¼	cup soy sauce
¼	cup canola oil
2	tablespoons Pommery or Dijon mustard
3	tablespoons freshly squeezed lemon juice (1 lemon)
4	chicken breast halves with bones

Mix first 4 ingredients in bowl and pour over chicken. Let marinate several hours or overnight.

Grill chicken or broil 15-20 minutes per side or until browned and cooked through.

Serve with rice and sautéed kale.

Serves 4

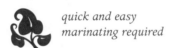

quick and easy
marinating required

Garlic Chicken

This is real comfort food, and not overly garlicky.

1	3-4 pound chicken
1	head garlic
½	cup kosher salt

Preheat oven to 375°.

Wash chicken and pat dry.

Separate and peel cloves of garlic. Place in food processor with kosher salt and puree until a paste forms. Add salt if too thin, but be sure to use kosher salt. Regular table salt will not work.

Rub paste all over chicken, inside and out. Place on a steel rack set over a pan with 1 cup water in it. Bake 1 hour. Remove crust.

Serve with mashed potatoes and fresh steamed vegetables.

Serves 4

easy

Cook's Tip:
Kosher salt, a coarser-grained salt than table salt, is usually additive free. Chefs often choose to use kosher salt for its texture and flavor.

Cook's Tip:
*This recipe is most
successful when
chicken breasts are
grilled. Chicken can
be sautéed although
the result will be
slightly different.*

Grilled Chicken with Raspberry Sauce

3   tablespoons soy sauce
½   cup sugar
⅔   cup raspberry vinegar
1   cup water
4   tablespoons frozen raspberries, thawed
2   tablespoons cornstarch, mixed with ⅓ cup water
4   boneless, skinless chicken breast halves, lightly
    seasoned and brushed with oil.

In saucepan, combine soy sauce, sugar, vinegar, water and raspberries. Bring to boil and reduce slightly. Add cornstarch mixture and cook briefly. Strain sauce to remove raspberry seeds. Keep sauce warm while grilling chicken until cooked through, about 7 minutes per side.

Serve chicken with sauce.

Serves 2-4

 *quick and easy*

Stir-Fry Chicken with Broccoli and Sweet Peppers

1   pound boneless chicken breasts, cut into strips
2   tablespoons oil
4   cups vegetables: broccoli flowerets, sweet pepper strips, sugar snap beans and sliced water chestnuts
1½   cups chicken broth
3   tablespoons soy sauce, light okay
2   tablespoons cornstarch
2   teaspoons brown sugar
1   garlic clove, crushed
1   tablespoon fresh grated ginger or ¾ teaspoon ground rice for 4 people

Stir fry chicken in hot oil in large skillet until browned. Add broccoli, pepper, sugar snap beans and water chestnuts. Stir fry until crisp-tender.

Mix broth, soy sauce, cornstarch, sugar, garlic and ginger. Add to skillet. Bring to boil and boil 1 minute.

Serve chicken and vegetables over rice.

Serves 4

 easy

Variations:
Feel free to play with your combinations of vegetables here. For instance, snow peas or sliced Japanese eggplant would work nicely.

Philippine Grilled Chicken

Recipes from the Philippines show a wonderful combination of Asian and Spanish influences.

4	chicken breast halves, bones in
¼	cup Hoisin sauce, available at most grocery stores
3	tablespoons ketchup
1	tablespoon white vinegar
1	tablespoon granulated sugar
¼	teaspoon garlic powder
1½	tablespoons soy sauce
1½	tablespoons dry white wine
	butter

Wash chicken thoroughly and set aside. Combine rest of ingredients except butter. Marinate chicken in sauce 1 hour.

Grill chicken over medium hot coals for about 15 minutes per side, basting with butter; or sauté over medium heat.

Boil leftover sauce over medium-high heat for 3 minutes if you wish to add to chicken prior to serving.

Serves 4

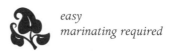
easy
marinating required

> "This is my grandfather's favorite quick way to make Chinese barbeque chicken breast. Philippine cooking is heavily influenced by our roots in China and Spain. The wine is the Spanish influence. Chinese do not use wine."
>
> *Lee Tolentino, Woodward parent*

Chicken Adobo

In the Philippines this is considered an everyday dish.

1	3-4 pound chicken, cut into serving pieces
3-4	garlic cloves, minced
½	cup soy sauce
⅓	cup vinegar
⅓	cup water
1	teaspoon coarsely ground black pepper
1-2	bay leaves
	orange slices

Arrange chicken in enamel or stainless steel pot. Combine rest of ingredients and add to chicken. Marinate 1 hour refrigerated.

Place pot over high heat. Bring to boil, then let simmer uncovered another 45 minutes to 1 hour, stirring occasionally, until done. Taste sauce and continue cooking a few minutes if needed to intensify flavor.

This dish keeps well in the refrigerator for several days. If refrigerated, reheat in microwave before serving.

Arrange chicken pieces around steamed basmati rice and pour sauce over. Garnish with orange slices.

Serves 4-6

 easy
can do ahead
marinating suggested

General Tso's Chicken

2	pounds boneless chicken thighs
1	egg white
2	tablespoons cornstarch
2	tablespoons soy sauce
2	tablespoons Hoisin sauce
2	tablespoons dark soy sauce, available at most supermarkets
2	tablespoons sugar
1	teaspoon salt
6	tablespoons chicken stock
1½	tablespoons cornstarch
	peanut oil for stir-frying
6	red chili peppers
2	teaspoons chopped garlic
2	tablespoons hot chili oil

Cut chicken into 1-inch cubes and put in glass bowl. Combine egg white, 2 tablespoons cornstarch and 2 tablespoons soy sauce. Pour over chicken cubes and toss until well coated.

Combine next 6 ingredients for seasoning mix and set aside.

In wok or frying pan, pour peanut oil 1-inch deep and heat to 300°. Fry chicken about 5 minutes, or until brown. Remove and drain. Discard oil.

Heat 2 tablespoons oil in wok. Add chili peppers and stir- fry briefly. Add garlic and chili oil and stir fry about 10 seconds.

Add seasoning mix and heat until sauce is boiling. Return chicken to wok and stir-fry until everything is heated through. Serve with white rice.

Serves 4

Cook's Tip

Hoisin sauce, also called Peking sauce, is a mixture of soybeans, garlic, chili peppers and spices. It is commonly used in Chinese cooking where it imparts a sweet, spicy flavor. It can usually be found in the oriental section of most large grocery stores.

Once opened, hoisin sauce can be stored in a glass container in the refrigerator almost indefinitely.

Peek a Blue Chicken

- 4 boneless, skinless chicken breast halves
- 2 teaspoons lemon juice
- ½ teaspoon seasoned salt
- ¼ teaspoon white pepper, divided
- 3 tablespoons unsalted butter

- ⅓ cup milk
- 1 tablespoon flour
- 1 ounce crumbled blue cheese
- 4 tablespoons butter
- ¼ teaspoon ground nutmeg
- ½ cup heavy cream
- 2 tablespoons finely chopped fresh parsley

On hard surface, pound breasts with mallet or similar flattening utensil until chicken is ¼ inch thick. Brush with lemon juice, sprinkle with salt and ⅛ teaspoon pepper.

In large frying pan, heat 3 tablespoons butter over medium heat. Add chicken and cook on each side until fork can be inserted with ease. Remove chicken from heat, cover and set aside.

To make sauce, mix milk and flour in small bowl until smooth. Over low heat, melt blue cheese, stirring constantly (add some pan drippings for added flavor if desired). Add flour mixture, butter, remaining pepper and nutmeg. Cook, stirring, 5 minutes or until sauce has thickened. Gradually stir in cream and 1 tablespoon parsley. Cook 1 minute longer.

Place pan with chicken over medium heat. Pour sauce over chicken and cook until done, about 10 minutes.

Serves 4

Variation:
You can lessen cholesterol and lighten this rich recipe with no loss of flavor by sautéing chicken breasts in olive oil instead of butter and replacing cream with skim milk for sauce. If using skim milk, you may want to thicken the sauce with a little flour as you would for white sauce.

Cook's Tip:
Whole, 2% and skim milk can almost always be used interchangeably in recipes despite the differences in fat content. Each will perform pretty much the same with only the expected decrease in richness when using 2% or skim. The exception would be most baked goods where the richness of the whole milk improves taste and texture.

Iced Tea

Whether you take your fried chicken with rice and gravy or with mashed potatoes on the side, you'll surely want iced tea to drink.

4 cups water
4 family size tea bags
⅓ cup sugar
1 bunch mint

Boil 4 cups water. Pour over sugar in ½-gallon container and stir to dissolve. Add mint and tea bags. Make sure bags are covered with water. Allow to steep 30 minutes to 1 hour. Remove tea bags and add water to make ½ gallon.

Barbeque Baked Chicken

When you're in the mood for barbeque in the middle of winter, this chicken will hit the mark.

¼ cup vinegar
2 teaspoons sugar
½ teaspoon pepper
¼ teaspoon red pepper
1 thick lemon slice
1 onion, peeled and sliced
½ cup water
1 tablespoon mustard
1½ teaspoons salt
¼ cup butter
½ cup ketchup
2 tablespoons Worcestershire sauce
6 chicken breast halves with bones in

Preheat oven to 350°.

Mix and simmer first 10 ingredients 20 minutes. Add ketchup and Worcestershire sauce and bring to boil.

Pour over chicken breasts. Bake 45 minutes to 1 hour. Keep covered for first ½ hour, then uncover and baste occasionally.

Serves 6

 easy

Classic Southern Fried Chicken

This is the standard by which all others are measured. The secret lies in the last step.

- 1   3-pound fryer, cut up
- ¾   cup buttermilk
- 2   cups all-purpose flour
- 1   teaspoon salt
- ½   teaspoon freshly ground white pepper
- 1   cup lard or vegetable shortening
- ½   cup water

Cut up fryer into 2 breasts, 2 thighs, 2 drumsticks and 2 wings plus giblets. Save backbone and any fat for chicken stock. Rinse pieces and giblets and pat dry. Sprinkle lightly with salt and pepper. Set aside for 15 minutes or seal in plastic bag overnight in refrigerator.

Place buttermilk in bowl. In second bowl, mix flour, 1 teaspoon salt and ½ teaspoon white pepper.

Dip chicken pieces and giblets quickly into buttermilk, then into flour. Make sure each piece is well covered with flour. Lay out all floured chicken pieces and giblets on tray.

In heavy 12-inch frying pan, heat lard to 375°. Temperature is crucial. It must be hot enough to make drop of water sizzle when dropped in pan.

A 12-inch frying pan should hold 8 pieces of chicken. Place large pieces in pan first, then fit smaller pieces around. Set aside giblets for now.

Cover frying pan, reduce heat to medium, and brown all pieces well on one side, 8-10 minutes. Turn pieces over, add giblets, cover and brown all pieces well again, 8-10 minutes.

Slowly and carefully add ½ cup water to chicken. Return cover and steam 5 minutes. Remove cover and turn pieces over once again to make crust crisp. Remove to warm platter.

Serves 4-6

 *can do ahead*

Fried Chicken Gravy

Make this gravy from the drippings after you've cooked fried chicken. The most important ingredient is what's left in the pan — all the little "crumbles" you can scrape up.

- 2   tablespoons lard
- 2   tablespoons all-purpose flour
- 2   cups water or chicken stock
       garlic powder to taste
       salt and black pepper to taste
       hot red pepper sauce to taste
       herbs to taste
       chicken "crumbles" scraped from pan after frying chicken

In the same pan you fried the chicken, melt lard and slowly add 2 tablespoons flour, stirring constantly. Stir flour while cooking for 10 minutes over very low heat, making a roux. Stir in water or chicken stock. Gravy should be smooth and brown. Add seasonings to taste. Last, add chicken "crumbles." Serve gravy over steamed rice, fried chicken itself (if you are feeling particularly indulgent) or biscuits.

Oven Chicken Kiev

Ginger Vinaigrette

½ cup vegetable oil
½ cup orange juice, preferably freshly squeezed
¼ cup honey
½ teaspoon salt
¼ cup fresh lemon juice
1 teaspoon finely chopped fresh ginger
¼ cup chopped fresh cilantro
¼ teaspoon cayenne pepper

Combine ingredients together in blender. Blend on high until mixture is well blended and a lovely green color. This vinaigrette is excellent on chicken, fish, or salad.

3 tablespoons butter, softened
1 teaspoon minced fresh parsley
¼ teaspoon garlic salt
1 cup cracker crumbs
⅛-¼ teaspoon seasoned salt
⅓ cup evaporated milk or whole milk
6 boneless, skinless chicken breast halves
2 tablespoons vegetable oil

Preheat oven to 425°.

Combine first 3 ingredients, mix well, and shape into small loaf resembling stick of butter. Cover and freeze until firm, about 45 minutes. Place each chicken breast half on sheet of waxed paper and flatten to ¼-inch thickness, using meat mallet or rolling pin. Cut butter mixture into 6 portions. Place 1 piece of butter in center of each breast half. Fold long sides of chicken over butter, fold ends over and secure with wooden pick.

Spread oil in 13x9x2-inch pan and set aside.

Combine cracker crumbs and seasoned salt. Dip each chicken roll into milk and coat with cracker crumbs.

Place chicken, seams side up, in prepared pan. Bake at 425° for 15 minutes. Carefully turn each piece. Bake another 5-10 minutes, until golden.

Serves 6

Red Snapper Fillets with Papaya Relish

Easy, elegant and delicious, this combination of fish fillets and colorful relish makes a lovely presentation.

3 pounds fresh fillets of red snapper, grouper, mahi mahi, amberjack or salmon
1 tablespoon olive oil
3 tablespoons Ginger Vinaigrette (page 146)
8 ounces grated fresh mozzarella cheese
⅓ cup sun-dried tomatoes in oil, cut in slivers

Preheat oven to 400°.

Pour olive oil in bottom of 9x13-inch baking pan. Place fillets in pan. Pour Ginger Vinaigrette over fish. Sprinkle mozzarella cheese and 6 to 8 sun-dried tomato slivers over each piece of fish. Bake uncovered at 400° for 15-20 minutes, or grill.

Serve on platter with Papaya Relish.

Serves 4-6

 easy

Papaya Relish

½ papaya, chopped
½ honeydew melon, chopped
1 pink grapefruit, chopped
½ cantaloupe, chopped
1 tablespoon capers, drained
1 jalapeño pepper, seeded and chopped
1 red pepper, diced
1 purple onion, chopped
1 tablespoon each, chopped fresh basil, mint and cilantro
3 tablespoons vinaigrette, preferably Ginger Vinaigrette
  salt and pepper to taste

Combine fruits, vegetables and herbs in order listed. Toss gently. Mix with desired amount of Ginger Vinaigrette. Salt and pepper to taste.

Salmon Fillets with Tri-Color Peppercorn Sesame Crust

4   skinless, boneless salmon fillets
1   tablespoon pink peppercorns
1   tablespoon green peppercorns
½   teaspoon cracked black pepper
½   cup sesame seeds
    juice of 1 lemon
¾   teaspoon dried dill weed
¼   teaspoon garlic powder
2   tablespoons butter
    salt

Preheat oven to 350°.

Crush peppercorns. Combine with black pepper and sesame seeds in small bowl and set aside.

Lightly grease casserole dish and arrange fillets in it. Pour lemon juice over fillets, then season with dill, garlic and salt.

Bake 15 minutes. Remove from oven and spread sesame mixture evenly over fillets. Dot with butter. Bake another 10 minutes or to desired degree of doneness.

Serves 4

"The outdoor grill has always been my favorite way to prepare fish, but in 1994 we had 21 consecutive days of rain in Atlanta, so I came up with this alternative, which Bon Appetit Magazine tested and accepted for its Cook's Exchange column."

*Patti Robbins,
Woodward parent*

Grilled Salmon with Cucumber Dill Sauce

¾ cup plain yogurt
⅓ cup mayonnaise, low-fat okay
½ cup seeded and coarsely chopped cucumber
¼ cup chopped fresh dill or 1 teaspoon dried
1 teaspoon grated fresh lemon zest
½ teaspoon salt
¼ teaspoon pepper

2 pounds salmon fillets
  salt and pepper to taste

To prepare sauce, mix first 7 ingredients and let stand at room temperature 15 minutes or refrigerate 1 hour. Can make a day ahead.

Heat grill very hot. Remove skin from salmon. Season with salt and pepper. Oil grill well to prevent fish from sticking. Grill 7 minutes each side, using frame or 2 spatulas to turn and lift fish.

Serve with fresh tomatoes and corn on the cob.

Serves 4

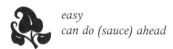 *easy*
can do (sauce) ahead

Creamy Tarragon Buttermilk Sauce

Delicious over grilled salmon, and over grilled vegetables too

4 teaspoons tarragon vinegar
¼ cup chopped fresh parsley
½ teaspoon dried tarragon leaves
2 green onions, chopped
½ cup low-fat buttermilk
¼ cup ricotta cheese
¼ cup low-fat cottage cheese
2 tablespoons fresh lemon juice
1 cup mayonnaise freshly ground black pepper

In blender, mix vinegar, parsley, tarragon and onion, blending until onion and parsley are minced. Add buttermilk, cheeses and lemon juice. Blend about 10 seconds. Add mayonnaise. Mix again until well blended. Refrigerate until ready to serve. Garnish with freshly ground black pepper.

Lime Cream Sauce

1   cup cream, half-
     and-half or milk
½   cup lime juice
1   teaspoon sugar
1   tablespoon
     reserved fish
     liquid or bottled
     clam juice
1   teaspoon dry
     crab boil
2   tablespoons
     softened butter
2   tablespoons
     all-purpose flour
     salt and freshly
     ground pepper
     hot pepper sauce

Heat cream and lime
juice but do not boil.
(If using half-and-half
or milk, the mixture
will curdle at this
point.) Add reserved
fish liquid and crab
boil. Combine softened
butter and flour into
paste and whisk into
sauce in small pieces to
thicken. Continue to
whisk until mixture is
smooth and just coats a
spoon. Taste and adjust
seasonings with salt,
pepper and hot sauce.

Yellow Tail Snapper with Lime Cream Sauce

1   3-pound yellow tail snapper or 2 1½-pound snappers
1   tablespoon olive oil
     salt and freshly ground pepper

Preheat oven to 450°.

Oil one large piece of aluminum foil per fish. Rub fish with olive oil and add salt and pepper inside and out. Lay fish on foil, bring ends together and roll down as you would a paper bag, pinching ends together to seal.

Place on cookie sheet and bake 12 minutes per inch of thickness, measured at thickest part of fish. Open package, drain off and reserve liquid.

This method can be used for any whole fish. Serve with Lime Cream Sauce.

Serves 4

 *quick and easy*

Swordfish au Poivre

One of the great fish recipes of all time

2 pounds swordfish (4 small steaks)
4 tablespoons crushed pink peppercorns
2 tablespoons unsalted butter
2 tablespoons vegetable oil
¼ cup pale dry sherry
1 cup heavy cream
½ teaspoon salt
1 tablespoon fresh lemon juice
3 tablespoons minced fresh parsley

Season swordfish lightly with salt, then press crushed peppercorns into both sides of steaks. Cover and refrigerate 1 hour.

In a large skillet, heat butter and oil. Add fish and cook 10 minutes for each inch of thickness, turning midway through cooking. Remove from pan and keep warm.

Pour excess oil and butter from pan and deglaze with sherry. Bring to boil. Add cream, salt, lemon juice. Simmer 2 to 3 minutes, stirring constantly. Taste for seasoning and adjust if necessary. Stir in parsley.

Serve fish masked with sauce. For an elegant dinner, accompaniments might include rice pilaf and steamed asparagus.

Serves 4

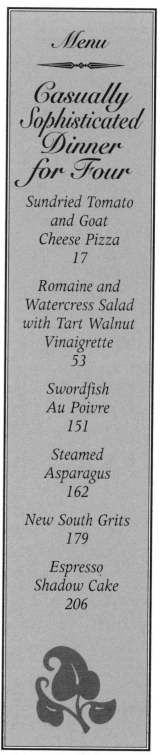

Menu

Casually Sophisticated Dinner for Four

Sundried Tomato
and Goat
Cheese Pizza
17

Romaine and
Watercress Salad
with Tart Walnut
Vinaigrette
53

Swordfish
Au Poivre
151

Steamed
Asparagus
162

New South Grits
179

Espresso
Shadow Cake
206

Ginger Steamed Striped Bass

Cook's Tip:

To deglaze a pan in which you have sautéed meat, chicken, fish, etc., remove excess fat, add a small portion of liquid, then heat, stirring to loosen bits of browned food that have stuck to the pan. You can then use the deglazed mixture as the base for sauce.

1	tablespoon vegetable oil
1	pound fresh striped bass fillets
½	cup sliced green onions
1	garlic clove, minced
1	cup sliced fresh mushrooms
2	tablespoons peeled and minced fresh ginger
¼	cup chicken stock
¼	cup dry white wine
4	teaspoons teriyaki sauce
1	tablespoon cornstarch
1	tablespoon water

fresh parsley sprigs
lemon slices

Heat oil in large sauté pan. Add fish and cook 1 minute. Turn pieces carefully with wide spatula. Sprinkle onions, garlic, mushrooms and ginger evenly over fish. Add stock, wine and teriyaki sauce. Cover and let steam about 10 minutes or until fish flakes when tested with fork.

Remove fish to warm platter and keep warm.

Combine cornstarch and water. Gradually stir into hot liquid. Cook, stirring, until sauce is slightly thickened. Pour sauce over fish.

Garnish fish with fresh parsley and lemon slices. Serve with steamed white rice flavored with teriyaki or soy sauce.

Serves 4

 easy

Perfect Maryland Crabcakes

  1   egg, well beaten
  ½   cup mayonnaise
  ½   teaspoon Worcestershire sauce
  1   tablespoon minced fresh parsley
1½   teaspoons seafood seasoning
  ½   teaspoon ground black pepper
  ½   teaspoon dry mustard
6-8   finely crumbled saltine crackers
  1   pound crabmeat, preferably lump or backfin
       butter, for sautéing

Combine all ingredients except crabmeat and butter. Gently fold crabmeat into mixture. Shape into patties. Melt butter and sauté patties until lace-edged and golden brown, about 5 minutes per side.

While crab cakes are often served atop rolls in other parts of the country as a sandwich, in Maryland they are traditionally served with saltine crackers accompanied by cocktail sauce or tartar sauce.

Makes 6-8 crab cakes

 *quick and easy*

Tarragon Tartar Sauce

  2   cups mayonnaise,
       low-fat okay
  ½   cup chopped
       fresh tarragon or
       2 tablespoons
       dried
  3   tablespoons
       finely minced
       green or
       red onion
  2   tablespoons fresh
       lemon juice
  2   tablespoons
       chopped capers
       salt and freshly
       ground pepper
       to taste

Combine all ingredients and chill at least 1 hour before serving.

Steamed Mussels in White Wine Sauce

Variation:

Eliminate cream for a lower-fat version that is still delicious.

2 pounds fresh mussels, washed and brushed thoroughly, beards removed (page 92)
1 teaspoon olive oil
½ cup diced fresh leek
4 shallots, finely chopped
3 garlic cloves, finely chopped
1 cup dry white wine
½ fresh chili pepper, seeded and finely chopped, or dash dried chili flakes
½ cup whipping cream, half-and-half or milk
    freshly ground black pepper

Heat olive oil in large pot. Add leeks, shallots, and garlic. Sauté quickly, about 1 minute, without letting ingredients color. Add white wine, chili and mussels to pot. Cover and steam on high heat for 2 minutes. Add cream and steam 2 more minutes.

Once mussels have opened, remove from pot and keep warm. Discard any that do not open. Reduce liquid in pot by half and pour over mussels.

Season with pepper and serve accompanied by fresh baguette.

Serves 2-4

 *quick and easy*

Spicy Shrimp with Lime and Sweet Salsa

½   cup fresh lime juice
4   garlic cloves, minced
½   cup coarsely chopped fresh mint
2   tablespoons Chinese sesame chili oil
1   pinch of cayenne pepper or to taste
32   medium-to-large raw shrimp, peeled and deveined, tails kept on
2   ripe mangoes, peeled and chopped
1½   cups hot salsa or enough to equal amount of chopped mango
2-3   cups cooked rice

Combine and mix lime juice, garlic, mint, sesame chili oil and cayenne pepper. Add shrimp and toss. Cover and refrigerate at least one hour.

In second bowl, combine chopped mango and salsa, cover and refrigerate until ready to serve.

When ready, remove shrimp from marinade and broil or grill 1-2 minutes on each side, just until pink. Do not overcook or shrimp will toughen.

Serve shrimp warm over rice with cold salsa .

Serves 4

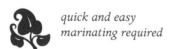 quick and easy
marinating required

Cook's Tip:
An easy method for marinating is to place ingredients in large airtight bag and refrigerate until ready to use.

Orange Ginger Sauce

1 cup orange marmalade
4 tablespoons fresh lemon juice
2 tablespoons fresh orange juice
1 tablespoon prepared horseradish
½ teaspoon ground ginger
½ teaspoon salt
½ teaspoon dried mustard

Combine and puree in food processor or blender.

Beer Batter Shrimp with Orange Ginger Sauce

1 can beer
1 cup all-purpose flour
1½ teaspoons salt
1½ teaspoons paprika

vegetable oil for frying
1 pound medium-to-large shrimp, peeled and deveined
¼ cup lemon juice
1 cup all-purpose flour for coating

Whisk together first 4 ingredients for beer batter. Set aside.

Pour vegetable oil into frying pan to a depth of 2 inches and heat to 375°, hot but not smoking.

Sprinkle shrimp with lemon juice. Coat with flour and dip into beer batter. Drop shrimp into hot oil and fry until golden brown.

Serve with Orange Ginger Sauce.

Serves 4

Low Country Shrimp

Messy but wonderful

2½	pounds raw shrimp in shells
¾	cup margarine
1½	teaspoons pepper
2	teaspoons dried rosemary or 4 teaspoons fresh
1	teaspoon dried thyme or 2 teaspoons fresh
2	teaspoons celery salt
½	teaspoon cayenne pepper
½	teaspoon Worcestershire sauce
1	teaspoon olive oil
	lemon juice to taste

Preheat oven to 450°.

Melt margarine. Add everything that follows and marinate shrimp
6 hours. Bake in 2-quart glass baking dish 20-30 minutes until shrimp
are pink.

To serve, line table with newspaper. Serve with green salad and French
bread. Peel, eat and sop up sauce with bread.

Serves 6

easy
marinating required

Hot Seafood Mousse with Shrimp Sauce

An impressive addition to a buffet

1	pound fresh scallops or sole
2	tablespoons melted butter
1	tablespoon all-purpose flour
1	egg, lightly beaten
	salt and white pepper, to taste
	dash nutmeg
2	cups half-and-half

¼	cup butter
¼	cup all-purpose flour
2¼	cups whole or 2% milk
3	tablespoons fresh lemon juice (1 lemon squeezed)
	white pepper
1	cup cooked shrimp, preferably salad shrimp

lemon slices
parsley

Preheat oven to 350°.

Finely chop scallops in blender or food processor. Add butter, flour, egg, salt, pepper and nutmeg. Process 30 seconds. With machine running, gradually add half-and-half.

Grease 4-cup mold with cooking spray and pour in scallop mixture. Cover with foil. Place in small roasting pan. Pour enough boiling water into roasting pan to come halfway up sides. Bake at 350° until toothpick inserted in center comes out clean, about 1 hour. Add more water, if necessary, to maintain consistent level.

Meanwhile make sauce. Melt butter in saucepan over medium heat. Stir in flour and cook for 1 minute. Whisk in milk. Bring to boil, stirring constantly. Reduce heat to low. Stirring constantly, cook for 5 more minutes, or until smooth. Sauce should coat back of spoon. Stir in lemon juice and pepper to taste. Add shrimp and heat through. Makes about 3 cups.

When mousse has finished baking, remove mold from water and let stand 10 minutes. Loosen edges of mousse with point of sharp knife. Invert heated platter over top and unmold.

Pour half of shrimp sauce over mousse. Garnish with lemon slices and parsley. Serve immediately, passing extra sauce separately.

Serves 6

Vegetables and Sides

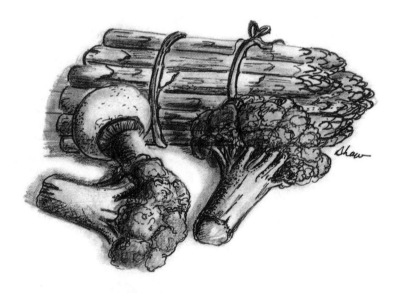

Vegetables and Sides

Mixed Grilled Vegetables

⅓ cup white balsamic vinegar
2 tablespoons olive oil
2 shallots, finely chopped
1 teaspoon dried Italian seasoning
¼ teaspoon salt
¼ teaspoon pepper
1½ teaspoons molasses

½ pound scraped carrots
1 sweet red pepper
1 sweet yellow pepper
2 zucchini
2 yellow squash
1 large onion
½ pound mushrooms

Combine first 7 ingredients for dressing and set aside.

Cut vegetables into large pieces and put in marinade/dressing. Stir to coat and let stand 30 minutes.

Drain vegetables and put in grill basket. If you have no basket, leave vegetables in large pieces and grill on rack so they cannot fall through. Cook over medium hot grill until done, turning occasionally, 10-20 minutes.

Cut vegetables into bite-size pieces and spoon dressing over. Serve warm or refrigerate over night.

Serves 4-6

   *can do ahead*

Vegetable Fajitas

Leftover grilled vegetables make great fajitas. On a warm flour tortilla, place a combination of shredded cheddar and Monterey Jack cheese. Layer on vegetables, salsa (page 26) and sour cream. Roll up and enjoy.

Easy Hollandaise

8 tablespoons butter, softened at room temperature
4 egg yolks
3 tablespoons lemon juice
pinch of cayenne
7 tablespoons hot water or less as needed
salt and white pepper to taste

In food processor or with beater, cream butter, adding egg yolks one at a time. Add lemon juice, pinch of cayenne and water and mix well.

Cook in double boiler over boiling water a few minutes until thick. Taste and add salt and white pepper as needed.

Serve over asparagus, broccoli or steamed vegetable of your choice.

Makes about 1 cup

Steamed Asparagus

When buying asparagus, it is not size that counts. Pencil thin asparagus will not necessarily be more tender than their fat friends. Tightly closed flower buds are the best indicator of fresh, flavorful asparagus.

1 lemon
1 teaspoon salt
1 pound trimmed asparagus
2 tablespoons melted butter

Heat 1 inch of water in 10-inch skillet. Add juice of half a lemon and 1 teaspoon salt; bring to a simmer. Add asparagus and simmer for about 8 minutes or until the spear can be easily pierced with the tip of a knife. Do not cook until limp.

Dress simply with a squirt of lemon juice and a bit of melted butter, though there are some among us whose idea of heaven is a plate of asparagus blanketed in hollandaise.

Serves 4-6

 easy

Cuban Black Beans

A traditional Cuban meal is black beans over white rice with roast pork.

1	pound dried black beans
8	cups water
1	large bell pepper, halved and seeded
2	tablespoons olive oil
1	large onion, chopped
1	large bell pepper, chopped
3	teaspoons salt
½	teaspoon freshly ground black pepper
1	teaspoon dried oregano
1	teaspoon sugar
2	tablespoons vinegar
2	tablespoons dry white wine or dry sherry

Rinse black beans. In large pot combine beans, water and halved bell pepper. Soak, covered, 8 hours or overnight. Or "quick soak" (page 73).

Bring to boil, reduce heat and simmer, covered, 1 hour, stirring occasionally. Discard bell pepper.

Heat oil in frying pan, add onions, garlic and chopped bell pepper. Sauté until vegetables are tender, then pour vegetables into bean pot. Add salt, pepper, oregano and sugar. Stir well and simmer, covered, 1 hour.

Add vinegar and wine and simmer for 1 more hour.

Serves 8-10

easy
can do ahead

Marinated Broccoli à la Greque

"This recipe came to me in a collection of 200 recipes my sister, Margaret Anne Watkins, gathered from family and friends as a shower gift when I was married in 1988."

Beth King,
Woodward Alumna

1	large bunch broccoli
1	teaspoon garlic powder
½	teaspoon dry mustard
⅓	cup vegetable oil
⅓	cup olive oil
½	teaspoon sugar
1	teaspoon onion powder
1	teaspoon dried oregano
½	teaspoon dried thyme
½	teaspoon pepper
⅓	cup vinegar
6	ounces feta cheese
1	cup pitted black olives
2	tomatoes

Steam broccoli.

While broccoli is steaming, whisk next 10 ingredients. Place steamed broccoli in large bowl and pour seasoning mixture over. This dish can be refrigerated at this point until ready to serve. If refrigerated, bring to room temperature before proceeding.

When ready to serve, drain broccoli and top with crumbled feta, black olives and quartered tomatoes.

Serves 6

Variation:

To turn into entree, double the recipe and serve over 8 ounces of linguini or extra thin spaghetti.

*quick and easy
do ahead*

Moroccan Carrots

If you don't believe carrots can taste exotic, as well as wonderful, try these and you'll change your mind.

1	pound carrots
3	tablespoons olive oil
1	tablespoon vinegar
2	garlic cloves, crushed
½	tablespoon cumin
½	tablespoon salt
1	teaspoon red pepper
½	teaspoon cayenne, or to taste

Peel carrots, clean and place in steamer. Cook until fork-tender, 5-8 minutes. Cool carrots to room temperature and cut into ¼-inch thick rounds.

Mix olive oil, vinegar, garlic and spices together. Combine in serving bowl with carrots. At this point, carrots can be refrigerated up to 4 days. They seem to get spicier over time.

Serve at room temperature with or before main dish.

Serves 4

 *quick and easy
can do ahead*

> *"This recipe came from a little town along the Atlantic coast of Morocco. This town, where I spent my childhood, was called Mogado. The recipe is at least 75 years old."*
>
> *Jacques Elfersy,
> Woodward parent*

Sautéed Kale

3	pounds kale, washed and with stems removed
2	tablespoons olive oil
1	tablespoon butter
2	garlic cloves, crushed
½	cup chicken stock
	salt and pepper to taste

Slice kale into ½-inch strips.

Heat oil and butter in large skillet. Sauté garlic briefly and add kale with a little chicken stock. Stir, then cover and cook over medium heat for 5-10 minutes, adding stock as needed to keep kale moist.

Season kale with salt and pepper and serve warm beside mustard soy chicken (page 137).

Serves 4

 *quick and easy*

Grilled Turkey Cutlets

Plan on 8 cutlets for 4 people. Season cutlets with salt and pepper to taste and grill for 2-4 minutes per side.

Quick Collard Greens in Shallot-Lemon Butter

Here is an elegant new version of greens that is also simple and quick to prepare.

1	bunch collard greens, washed, stemmed, and julienned
6	cups chicken broth
	salt to taste

1	cup unsalted butter
⅓	cup minced shallots
1	garlic clove, minced or pushed through a press
2	teaspoons lemon juice
	salt to taste

Bring broth to boil and add collards and salt as desired. Cook 5-10 minutes until just tender.

Melt ¼ cup butter in saucepan, add shallots and garlic, then sauté until shallots are translucent. Whisk remaining butter into pan 1 tablespoon at a time until all is incorporated. Remove from heat immediately and add lemon juice. Salt to taste.

Pour shallot-lemon butter over collards and grilled turkey cutlets. Serve with corn pudding (below).

Serves 4

 easy

Corn Pudding

4¼	cups fresh corn (thawed if frozen, drained if canned)
¼	cup sugar
¼	cup sifted flour
1	teaspoon salt
¼	teaspoon black pepper
2	eggs, beaten
2	tablespoons melted butter
1½	cups milk

Preheat oven to 350°.

Mix together corn, sugar, flour, salt, and pepper. Add beaten eggs and melted butter. Add milk. Mix well and pour into well greased 1½-quart casserole. Bake about 1 hour at 350°, or until light brown on top.

Serves 6

easy
can do ahead

Dhal

This dish of seasoned lentils is a staple of Indian menus.

2	tablespoons vegetable oil
2	medium onions, finely chopped
2	rounded teaspoons turmeric
½	teaspoon ground ginger
1	teaspoon salt
8	whole cloves
½	cinnamon stick
1	large bay leaf
1	teaspoon garam masala (page 76)
2	teaspoons curry powder
6	whole green cardamoms
¼	teaspoon chili powder
1	8-ounce package green lentils, washed several times
¼	cup chopped fresh cilantro

Sauté onion in approximately 2 tablespoons vegetable oil until transparent. Stir in spices, all at once, and sauté briefly. Remove from heat, add lentils, then return to heat and sauté briefly. Add water to cover well.

Simmer, uncovered, on low. Pot must be watched carefully and water added from time to time. After about 10 minutes, add cilantro, partially cover pot and simmer gently for ½ hour. Add water, as necessary, to obtain desired consistency.

Serve with Chicken Korma (page 80) or other curry along with basmati rice and naan bread (page 251).

Serves 8-10

 *can do ahead*

Bourbon Mushrooms

Variations:

Serve with toothpicks as an hors d'oeuvre or on a sliced baguette with plenty of sauce as a first course.

2	tablespoons butter
2	tablespoons olive oil
2	garlic cloves, minced
1	pound fairly large mushrooms, cleaned and stemmed
⅔	cup minced ham
3	tablespoons minced fresh shallots
¼	cup bourbon
6	tablespoons minced fresh parsley
½	teaspoon dried thyme
1	tablespoon Dijon mustard
1	cup beef broth
3	tablespoons heavy cream (skim milk will work)
	salt and white pepper to taste

fresh thyme or parsley

Melt butter with olive oil in large heavy skillet. Add garlic and brown mushrooms in several batches, sautéing briefly at high temperature. Transfer to bowl.

In same skillet, over low to medium heat, cook ham, shallots, and bourbon until bourbon is reduced to a glaze. Add remaining ingredients and cook until liquid reduces to nice thickness and flavors are developed, about 5-10 minutes. Taste and adjust seasonings.

Return mushroom mixture to sauce and cook on low heat a few minutes, until fully cooked. Transfer to chafing dish or plate. At this point you can refrigerate up to 2 days and heat through before serving garnished with thyme or parsley. These are nice alongside any simple meat or poultry dish.

Serves 8

easy
can do ahead

Deep Fried Okra

Another Southern classic beloved for its crunchy yet soft consistency

1	**pound okra**
½	**egg, beaten**
1	**tablespoon water**
1	**cup buttermilk**
1	**cup all-purpose flour**
1	**cup cracker meal**
1	**teaspoon salt**
½	**teaspoon freshly ground white pepper**
2	**cups vegetable oil**

Wash and trim okra, then slice into ¼-inch pieces.

Mix egg, water and buttermilk in bowl.

In separate bowl prepare seasoned flour by mixing flour, cracker meal, salt and pepper.

Put okra slices into buttermilk wash. Lift out with slotted spoon and drain well. Place in seasoned flour and shake. Take out and place on cake rack and knock off excess flour.

Drop in batches into hot oil until golden brown, about 2-3 minutes. Drain on paper towels. Serve immediately.

Serves 4-6

 easy

Ratatouille

Variation:

For a vegetarian luncheon dish, add ¼ cup Parmesan cheese to ratatouille and combine. Place into 4 individual gratin dishes and top each with ¼ cup shredded mozzarella or fontina cheese. Place in 450° oven until top is golden.

2 tablespoons olive oil
1 large purple onion, thinly sliced
2 garlic cloves, crushed
1 red or green bell pepper, thinly sliced
1 medium eggplant or 2 zucchini or a combination of both
2 ripe tomatoes, cubed
¼ teaspoon dried basil
¼ teaspoon dried oregano
1 tablespoon balsamic vinegar
   salt and freshly ground black pepper to taste

Peel eggplant and slice. Sprinkle with salt and drain in colander for 1 hour. Rinse, pat dry, and cut in cubes.

Heat oil, add onion and garlic, and sauté until onion is translucent. Do not brown. Add bell pepper, eggplant and/or zucchini. Cover and simmer over low heat for 15 minutes.

Add tomatoes and herbs and continue to cook uncovered another 10 minutes. Add salt and pepper and balsamic vinegar, 1 teaspoon at a time, tasting for correct seasoning.

Serves 4

*easy
can do ahead*

Rotkraut

This wintery combination of apples and red cabbage makes a colorful addition to the table on chilly nights.

- 6 slices bacon, cut into small pieces
- 3 tablespoons butter
- ½ cup chopped onion
- 3 pounds shredded red cabbage
- 2 medium Granny Smith apples, peeled and cut in small slices
- 1 small bay leaf
- 4 whole cloves
- 1 beef bouillon cube mixed with ½ cup water or ½ cup beef broth plus slightly more if needed
- 5 tablespoons red wine vinegar
- ½ cup red wine
- 2 tablespoons flour
- ½ cup water plus a little extra
  salt and pepper to taste

Fry bacon in heavy skillet. Drain skillet and add butter and onion and sauté. Add shredded cabbage and apples. Cover and shake skillet so fat coats cabbage. Add small quantity of beef broth to prevent sticking. Add bay leaf, cloves and bouillon. Cook 15 minutes, then add vinegar and 2½ tablespoons red wine.

Cook 30-40 minutes until cabbage is done.

Mix flour with beef broth and stir into cabbage. Add rest of wine and salt and pepper to taste.

Best when made a few days before serving. Refrigerate and heat through before offering alongside pork or beef roast and roasted potatoes.

Serves 10-12

 *easy
do ahead*

Squash Casserole

6-8 medium yellow squash
2½ cups chopped onion, preferably Vidalia
1 cup grated sharp cheddar cheese
½ cup sour cream, low-fat okay
2 tablespoons butter
    salt and pepper to taste
1 egg, beaten
2 tablespoons chopped fresh chives
¾ cup bread crumbs

Preheat oven to 350°.

Boil onions and squash until tender. Drain and add cheese and sour cream with butter. Salt and pepper to taste. Stir until melted. Remove from heat. Add egg and chives and stir well.

Pour into lightly greased 9x11-inch glass casserole dish. Sprinkle with bread crumbs and spray crumbs with cooking spray. Bake at 350° until browned, about 30 minutes.

Serves 6-8

easy
can do ahead

Baked Tomato Cups Dijon

Great with egg dishes as well as meats

6	medium tomatoes, halved crosswise
¼	cup Dijon mustard
¼	teaspoon salt
¼	cup plus 2 tablespoons seasoned breadcrumbs
¼	cup plus 2 tablespoons grated Parmesan cheese
¼	cup melted butter
1	tablespoon minced chopped parsley
⅛	teaspoon ground red pepper

Preheat oven to 350°.

Lightly brush cut surface of tomato halves with mustard. Place tomato halves, cut side up, in 13x9x2-inch baking dish and sprinkle with salt.

Combine breadcrumbs and remaining ingredients in small bowl and stir well. Top each tomato half with 1 tablespoon crumb mixture, spreading evenly. Bake at 350° for 10 minutes or until tomatoes are thoroughly heated and cheese melts.

Place tomatoes under broiler and broil 2-3 minutes or until tops are golden.

Serve with steak, tenderloin, or fish.

12 servings

 easy

Green Tomato Pie

3 medium green tomatoes
1 9-inch pie shell
  salt and pepper to taste
¾ cup mayonnaise
1 cup shredded cheddar cheese
¼ cup chopped onion
  dash of hot red pepper sauce
½ cup bread crumbs
1 tablespoon melted butter

Preheat oven to 350°.

Slice and peel green tomatoes. Blot tomatoes and place half of them in pie shell. Sprinkle with salt and pepper.

Combine mayonnaise, cheese, onion and hot red pepper sauce, stirring well. Spread half of mixture over tomato slices. Repeat with remaining tomatoes and mixture. Combine bread crumbs and melted butter and sprinkle over pie.

Bake in 350° oven for 40-45 minutes, or until crust is browned. Let stand about 15 minutes before serving.

Serves 6-8

 easy

Zucchini and Carrot Strands

Healthy, colorful and delicious

Vegetable cooking spray
2 medium carrots, peeled and cut into julienne strips 2½ inches long
¼ cup chicken broth
1 medium zucchini, cut into julienne strips 2½ inches long
1 garlic clove, or more to taste, minced
¼ teaspoon salt
⅛ teaspoon freshly ground pepper

Coat large non-stick skillet with cooking spray and place over medium heat until hot. Add carrots and sauté 1 minute.

Add chicken broth. Cook 1 minute, stirring occasionally. Stir in zucchini, garlic, salt and pepper. Cover and cook 3 minutes or until vegetables are crisp tender.

Serves 4

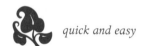 *quick and easy*

Zwiebelkuchen

This German onion pie makes a flavorful addition to a luncheon menu.

1	sheet frozen puff pastry, thawed according to package directions
2½	pounds yellow onions, thinly sliced
8	strips bacon, chopped and fried crisp
1¼	cups sour cream
4	eggs
5	tablespoons flour
¼	teaspoon caraway seed
	salt to taste

Preheat oven to 425°.

Flour working surface and roll out puff pastry to fit 10-inch greased spring form pan or large deep dish pie pan. Form pastry in pan bottom and up the sides.

Sauté onions 2-5 minutes without browning. Mix cooked bacon with sour cream, eggs, flour, caraway seed and salt. Fold gently into onions. Spread filling evenly on pastry and bake at 425° until golden brown, approximately 1 hour.

Serve warm.

Serves 6-8

New Potatoes Bavarian Style

2	shallots
½	cup butter
15	new red potatoes
1	tablespoon fresh rosemary
	pinch of salt
12	ounces German or German-style beer

Sauté shallots in butter in large pot for two minutes. Add potatoes and remaining ingredients to pot. Bring to boil, then lower heat and simmer, covered, 25 minutes. Keep an eye on simmering beer; if it starts to run dry, add small amount of water.

Remove lid and boil down liquid until thick. Cut potatoes in half with spatula while stirring and coating in pot with liquid.

Remove and serve. This is particularly good with spicy fish and chicken dishes.

Serves 6

easy

Rosemary Potatoes

2½ pounds potatoes
1-2 garlic cloves, chopped
1 tablespoon fresh rosemary
2 tablespoons olive oil
   salt and pepper to taste

Preheat oven to 400°.

Slice potatoes into ¼-inch rounds or as French fries. Place garlic, rosemary, olive oil, salt and pepper in large bowl and stir. Add potatoes and toss until coated.

Spread seasoned potatoes on cookie sheet sprayed with non- stick spray. Bake at 400° until golden brown, 30-40 minutes.

Serves 4

 easy

Variation:

If rosemary is unavailable, consider replacing with 1 teaspoon chili powder.

Sweet Potato Casserole

Only in the sweets-loving South would this casserole be considered anything but dessert.

4 cups cooked, mashed sweet potatoes
½ cup sugar
½ cup butter
2 eggs, lightly beaten
1 teaspoon vanilla extract
⅓ cup milk

⅓ cup melted butter
1 cup light brown sugar
½ cup all-purpose flour
1 cup chopped pecans

Preheat oven to 350°.

Mix sweet potatoes with sugar, butter, eggs, vanilla and milk. Place in buttered 13x9-inch baking dish.

Mix together topping ingredients and crumble over potatoes.

Bake in 350° oven for 25 minutes, or until top is brown and crunchy.

Serves 8

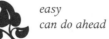 *easy*
can do ahead

Garlic Mashed Potatoes

> 2   pounds baking potatoes, peeled and quartered
> 1   head garlic, cloves separated and peeled
> ⅓   cup butter
> ½   cup half-and-half or milk, warmed
>   salt and pepper to taste

Place potatoes and garlic cloves in large pot of boiling salted water. Boil gently until potatoes and garlic can be easily pierced with fork.

Drain and return potatoes and garlic to pot. Add as much butter as your conscience will allow. Mash with potato masher or fork. Add half-and-half or milk to desired consistency. Season with salt and pepper. Great with any simple chicken or beef dish.

Serves 6

easy
can do ahead

Down Home Spoon Bread

More pudding than bread, this dish is usually eaten with a fork or a spoon.

> 1½   cups water
> 1   teaspoon salt
> 1   cup corn meal
> 2   tablespoons butter
> 1   cup milk
> 2   eggs, separated and beaten

Preheat oven to 350°.

Bring water and salt to boil in medium saucepan. Gradually stir in corn meal. Cook, stirring, until smooth. Add butter, milk, and well-beaten egg yolks. Mix well. Fold in 2 stiffly beaten egg whites.

Pour into greased 8x8-inch baking dish. Bake until firm, 30- 45 minutes.

Serves 3-4

easy

New South Grits

A sophisticated update with sundried tomatoes

- 4 **cups chicken stock**
- 1 **large garlic clove, split**
- 1 **cup yellow stone ground grits**
- 1 **tablespoon butter**
- ½ **cup grated fontina cheese**
- ¼ **cup sundried tomatoes in oil, drained and chopped**
  salt and freshly ground pepper to taste

Place stock with split garlic clove in medium saucepan and bring to boil. Lower heat, cover and simmer 10 minutes. Return to boil and slowly add grits, stirring to prevent lumps. Add butter. Lower heat and simmer, covered, for 20-25 minutes, stirring every 5 minutes or so. Cook until smooth and creamy.

Remove from heat and fish out garlic. Add cheese and stir until melted. Stir in sundried tomatoes. Taste and season as needed (if using canned stock, you may not need additional salt).

If not serving immediately, place the covered pan over simmering water or transfer grits to double boiler until ready to use.

Serve as a side dish in place of potatoes with chicken or pork. Or serve with grilled shrimp, a Carolina favorite.

Serves 6

easy
can do ahead

Variations:
You can use quick grits; just reduce cooking time to 8-10 minutes. You can substitute other cheeses for fontina. Gorgonzola, cheddar or any good melting cheese will work.

Winter Fruit Compote

2 cups grapefruit sections
2 cups orange or tangerine sections, pitted
1 cup pineapple chunks
2 cups sliced pears
2 cups sliced apple
1 cup red grapes
1 cinnamon stick
¾ cup sugar or to taste
¾ cup apricot brandy or orange juice

Combine fruits in serving bowl. Add cinnamon stick. In small bowl, mix together sugar and brandy. Toss fruit with sugar-brandy and marinate overnight.

Serves 10-12

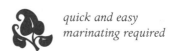

*quick and easy
marinating required*

Down Home Cornbread Dressing with Oysters (or without)

Every Southern family has its cornbread dressing recipe, to be made separately while the turkey is roasting.

4	cups crumbled cornbread
4	cups toasted French or good white bread cubes
½	cup melted butter
1	large onion, chopped
1	cup chopped celery
4	cups rich turkey or chicken stock
3	eggs, beaten
½	teaspoon freshly ground pepper
1½	teaspoons salt
1	teaspoon sage, optional
½	pint oysters or more to taste, optional
2	tablespoons turkey stock
2	tablespoons melted butter

Preheat oven to 350°.

Mix breads in large bowl. In skillet, sauté onion and celery in ½ cup butter. Add to breads with stock, eggs and seasonings. Pour into greased 9x12x2-inch baking dish. Bake 35-45 minutes at 350°. Halfway through baking, baste top with 2 tablespoons melted butter mixed with 2 tablespoons stock.

If adding oysters, remove pan from oven after 20 minutes, poke drained oysters into partially cooked dressing. Oysters can be put in only one side of dressing if some family members prefer plain dressing. Return to oven and complete cooking.

Serves 8

*easy
can do ahead*

Cook's Tip:

To toast bread cubes, place in single layer in 350° oven 10-15 minutes.

Variation:

For a barely sweet, slightly nutty dressing, use crumbled cranberry cornbread (page 252) and eliminate oysters.

Cook's Tip:

Cranberries can be found in stores for only a short time around the Thanksgiving and Christmas holidays; but you don't have to be limited by this. Cranberries can be frozen in the bag they come in for up to a year. To use, partially thaw and stir into muffins, breads or any other recipe that calls for cranberries. They really are too good to eat only once a year.

Baked Apples Stuffed with Sausage and Cranberries

A lovely accompaniment for poultry or game

1	pound bulk sausage
1	onion, chopped
1	teaspoon dried sage
1	teaspoon crumbled dried thyme
1	cup cranberries, picked over
½	cup fresh bread crumbs
3	ribs celery, chopped fine (about 1 cup)
½	cup fresh minced parsley
8	Golden Delicious apples

fresh sage leaves

Preheat oven to 375°.

Cook sausage, crumbled, over moderate heat in large skillet. Stir in onions, dried sage, thyme and cranberries. Add salt and pepper to taste if desired. Cook, stirring, until berries begin to pop. Stir in bread crumbs, celery and parsley. Remove from heat. (This step can be done up to 1 day in advance of baking apples. Refrigerate until ready to proceed.)

Cut off ½-inch top of apples. Reserve tops. Core apples. Scoop out and chop apple meat. Add chopped apple to stuffing.

Stuff apples, replace tops and arrange in baking dish. Pour 1 inch of hot water into pan and cover tightly with foil. Bake in 375° oven, 1½ hours.

Serve garnished with sage leaves if available.

Serves 8

 *can do partially ahead*

Cranberry Chutney

4	cups fresh cranberries
½	cup vinegar
¼	cup fresh lemon juice
1	cup seedless raisins
¼	cup thinly sliced crystallized ginger
⅓	cup chopped onion
1	tablespoon salt
1	teaspoon ground allspice
½	teaspoon ground cinnamon
½	teaspoon ground cloves
½	teaspoon ground ginger
1	1¾ ounce box dried fruit pectin
¾	cup packed dark brown sugar
4½	cups sugar (2 pounds)
10	½-pint jars, washed in dishwasher

Grind cranberries coarsely in food processor and place in large soup pot. Add vinegar, lemon juice, raisins, ginger, onion, salt, and spices. Mix well. Add pectin and stir.

Place pot over high heat. Stir until rolling boil forms. Add sugars at once and stir. Bring to rolling boil again and boil hard 5 minutes, stirring constantly.

Remove from heat. With spoon, skim off foam and discard. Ladle chutney into hot jars. Seal and turn upside down for 15 minutes to help tops seal. Turn right side up and cool.

Serve over brie cheese with crackers or with meats.

Makes 8-10 pints

easy
can do ahead

> **Cook's Tip:**
> *A rolling boil is a boil that cannot be stirred down.*

Baked Cranberry Sauce

In this deliciously different adaptation of the holiday standby, the berries stay whole in the thickened sauce to create a firm consistency.

   4   cups fresh cranberries
   1   cup sugar
   ½   teaspoon ground cinnamon, optional
   1   13-ounce jar orange marmalade
   3   tablespoons lemon juice
   1   cup coarsely chopped toasted walnuts

Preheat oven to 350°.

Wash and drain cranberries. Place in large bowl. Combine sugar with cinnamon, if desired, and add to cranberries, mixing well.

Spoon into 9-inch square pan and cover with aluminum foil. Bake at 350° for 45 minutes. Remove from oven and add marmalade and lemon juice, mixing well. Store in refrigerator or freeze. Add toasted walnuts just before serving.

Makes about 2½ cups

easy
can do ahead
can freeze

Pineapple Casserole

1   20-ounce can pineapple chunks with 3 tablespoons
      juice reserved
¼   cup sugar
2   tablespoons flour
1½   cups shredded cheddar cheese
      vegetable cooking spray
¼   cup melted butter
1   cup buttery cracker crumbs

Preheat oven to 350°.

Drain pineapple, reserving 3 tablespoons of juice. Combine sugar with flour and stir into reserved juice. Add cheese and pineapple chunks, mixing well. Cover flat, 1-quart casserole dish with cooking spray. Spoon in mixture.

Combine melted butter and cracker crumbs. Sprinkle over pineapple mixture. Bake at 350° until crumbs are lightly browned, 20-30 minutes.

Serves 8

easy
can do ahead

"I had a pineapple casserole recipe in the first Woodward Cookbook, but this one is 'new and improved.'"

*Beth Widener,
Woodward parent
and staff member*

Rutabaga and Apple Sauce

With its light delicate taste, this makes a wonderful, slightly different Thanksgiving side dish. For those unfamiliar with them, rutabagas resemble turnips and are a cross of turnip and cabbage.

2	large Granny Smith apples
½	teaspoon slivered lemon peel
¼	cup packed dark brown sugar
½	teaspoon cinnamon
1	tablespoon dark rum
1	tablespoon butter
½	pound rutabaga
2	tablespoons butter, softened
½	cup heavy cream
	salt and pepper to taste

Prepare applesauce. Peel, core and slice apples. Place apples with cinnamon, lemon and sugar in pot. Cook, covered, over low heat about 30 minutes, stirring occasionally, until apples are soft. Remove from heat. Mash and stir in butter and rum. This can be done in advance.

Preheat oven to 350°.

Peel and cube rutabaga; boil until tender. While still warm, mash rutabaga with butter and cream.

Beat in applesauce. Bake in 350° oven until heated through, about 15 minutes.

Serve with turkey or pork roast.

Serves 8-10

Desserts
Desserts
Desserts

Desserts, Desserts, Desserts

Old Fashioned Peach Cobbler

½ cup butter
6 cups ripe peaches, about 6-8 peaches, peeled and sliced
½ cup sugar, or more depending on peaches' sweetness

1 cup self-rising flour
1 cup sugar
1 cup buttermilk
½ teaspoon almond extract
½ teaspoon vanilla extract

Preheat oven to 350°.

Place ½ cup butter in glass 8x12-inch or 9x14-inch pan and put in oven.

Combine peaches and ½ cup sugar. Stir and allow to sit while you prepare batter. Juice will form.

To make batter, combine flour, 1 cup sugar, buttermilk and extracts. Stir with wire whisk until smooth.

Retrieve pan from oven. Pour batter over hot butter in pan. Do NOT stir. Pour peaches with juice over batter. Do NOT stir. Bake at 350° in top third of oven until bubbly and browned, 40-45 minutes.

Serves 8-10

 easy

Variations:

You can use 6 cups of any juicy fruit or combination of fruits, such as blackberries and nectarines or blueberries and peaches. You can also make with homemade chunky applesauce, in which case omit almond extract and add ½ teaspoon cinnamon. Or for a slightly different edge to the flavor, replace almond extract with brandy extract.

Variation:

To make into a festive holiday dessert, add ¼ cup cranberries and ¼ cup butterscotch chips to apples.

Cook's Tip:

Firm textured, tart apples are best for baking. Choose Winesap, Golden Delicious, Granny Smith, Rome Beauty or Northern Spy for apples to hold their shape during cooking. Using more than one variety of apple in a recipe gives the dish a more interesting flavor.

Autumn Apple Crisp

The topping forms a lovely, almost brittle shell over the apples that sets this luscious dessert apart from your usual crisps.

1	**cup sugar**
½	**cup butter**
¾	**cup flour**
1	**teaspoon cinnamon**
6	**tart apples, peeled and coarsely chopped**

Preheat oven to 350°.

Place chopped apples in greased 9x9-inch baking dish or 10-inch pie plate.

Combine sugar, flour and cinnamon in mixing bowl, cut in butter with pastry blender or by rubbing butter into flour and sugar with your fingers until mixture is crumbly. Pack mixture over top of apples.

Bake in 350° oven until top is brown, 40-45 minutes. Serve with vanilla or cinnamon ice cream, or with cream poured over top of each serving.

Serves 8-10

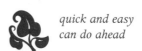

quick and easy can do ahead

Apple Custard Tart in Shortbread Crust

2   cups pastry flour
½   cup powdered sugar
1   cup butter
1   teaspoon vanilla

2   medium Granny Smith apples
2   tablespoons brown sugar
1   teaspoon cinnamon or 1 cinnamon stick
1   tablespoon butter
2   ounces apricot brandy
½   cup vanilla custard (page 200)

Preheat oven to 375°.

In food processor, blend flour, sugar and vanilla. Add butter by tablespoons through feed tube while machine is running. A ball of soft dough will form in machine. Refrigerate dough until slightly chilled, 20-30 minutes.

Grease 7-8-inch tart pan with cooking spray. Press dough into pan beginning with sides first and then filling in bottom of pan. Gently prick dough with fork. Bake at 375° until lightly browned, about 15-20 minutes.

Meanwhile peel and slice apples to approximately ¼-inch thickness. Mix together brown sugar, cinnamon and butter. In skillet, sauté apple slices in butter mixture 3-4 minutes. Add brandy (watch for flames) and simmer uncovered until apples are tender and sauce is reduced to 2 tablespoons. Remove cinnamon stick if using.

After crust has cooled slightly, fill with custard. (If using our custard recipe, you can make ¼ of the recipe.) Layer apples neatly around perimeter of tart overlapping slightly. Drizzle remaining liquid over tart.

Serve warm.

Serves 6-8

Cook's Tip:
3 medium-sized apples equal about 1 pound or 3 cups sliced or chopped.

Blue Ribbon Pie

This pie took first place at the Gwinnett County, Georgia, Fair in 1987! The trick is to use margarine, not butter, in the crust and to work fast according to blue ribbon winner and Woodward parent Moira Busby.

2½ cups all-purpose flour
1 cup cold margarine
   ice water
   waxed paper

3 cups fresh blueberries
2 cups fresh sliced peaches
1½ cups sugar
½ cup flour
2 teaspoons cinnamon

Preheat oven to 375°.

Mix flour with margarine by quickly, but gently, crumbling cold, hard margarine into flour with fingers. Leave chunks of margarine no larger than small grapes. Speed is everything.

Dribble cold water into flour mixture, tossing gently with fork, working fast. Add enough water so ball forms without being sticky. Wrap in waxed paper and chill in refrigerator at least 30 minutes.

Meanwhile, prepare filling, mixing all ingredients in large bowl. Let sit at least 20 minutes.

Divide crust into 2 pieces and pat into disks. On floured countertop, roll disks out fast, using minimum strokes, into 12-inch rounds. Flour liberally to keep from sticking.

Place bottom crust in 10-inch deep dish glass pie pan and fill with fruit mixture. Place top crust over filling and crimp edges firm and fast. Slit top with knife. At this point you can freeze raw pie, wrapped in waxed paper and foil, for up to 4 months.

Place pan under pie pan to catch drippings and bake on second rack in 375° oven for 30-40 minutes or until crust is brown and filling is bubbling.

Cool at least 1 hour before serving with vanilla ice cream.

Makes 1 pie

*quick and easy
can freeze*

Cook's Tip:
This recipe for pie crust will work well for any fruit pie.

Variations:
To make this a blackberry pie, substitute 5 cups of blackberries for blueberries and peaches, reduce cinnamon to ½ teaspoon and use a lattice crust. For lattice crust, roll out second crust and cut into 1-inch strips to place lattice-fashion over filling.

Brandy Tart

A South African winter dessert for a cold night around the fire

10	ounces pitted dates
1	teaspoon baking soda
1	cup boiling water
½	cup butter
1	cup sugar
1	jumbo egg, room temperature
1¼	cups all-purpose flour
	pinch of salt
½	teaspoon baking powder
¾	cup sugar
¾	cup water
1	teaspoon butter
1	teaspoon vanilla
½	cup brandy
	whipped cream as garnish

Preheat oven to 350°.

Sprinkle dates with baking soda. Pour boiling water over dates and leave to cool.

Cream butter and sugar in mixing bowl. (In winter, first rinse the bowl with hot water and dry.) When butter mixture is light and creamy, gradually beat in egg.

Sift flour, salt and baking powder 2 or 3 times. Alternately fold dry ingredients and date mixture into creamed mixture using a metal spoon. Pour into greased 10-inch pie or cake pan and bake for 45 minutes at 350°.

While tart is baking, prepare sauce. Bring sugar, water and butter to boil in small saucepan. Remove from heat and add vanilla and brandy.

Pour warm sauce over hot cake as it comes out of oven. Cool to room temperature. Flavor improves if tart is made 1 day before serving.

Serve with whipped cream.

Serves 10-12

*do ahead
can freeze*

Lemon Meringue Pie

Don't look for condensed milk in this Yankee style lemon pie recipe.

7	egg yolks
1¼	cups sugar
4	tablespoons cornstarch
1	pinch salt
1½	cups water
½	cup fresh lemon juice
1	tablespoon fresh lemon rind
7	egg whites
7	tablespoons sugar
	pinch of salt
1	baked 10-inch deep pie crust

Preheat oven to 350°.

Blend together first 4 ingredients. Add water, lemon juice and rind. Cook over very low heat, stirring constantly, until a pudding-like consistency is reached. Do not overcook. Set aside.

In large bowl, beat egg whites with sugar and salt, adding sugar gradually after whites are almost firm. Continue beating until stiff peaks form.

Fold ¼ of beaten egg whites into lemon mixture and fill pie crust. Gently cover with remaining meringue. Brown in 350° oven 10 minutes. This pie is best served the day it is baked, although it will keep refrigerated 1-2 days.

Serves 8-10

Cook's Tip:

When making meringue pies, make sure meringue touches pie shell all around to keep meringue from shrinking. Also, meringue placed on a hot filling will not form the wet layer between filling and meringue.

Cook's Tip:

To ensure you always have fresh lemon juice on hand, simply cut fresh lemons in half, place in plastic freezer bag, and freeze. Allow lemon halves to defrost overnight before juicing.

Coconut Custard Pie

Easy and delicious, this pie is also not as high in fat content as most of its peers.

- 1 cup sugar
- 1 teaspoon vanilla
- 1 tablespoon melted butter
- 1 cup loosely packed sweetened coconut
- 1 tablespoon self-rising flour
- ¾ cup buttermilk
- 3 eggs

- 1 unbaked pie crust

Preheat oven to 450°.

Mix all ingredients together. Pour into unbaked pie crust. Bake at 450° for 15 minutes, then at 350° for 15 minutes more.

Serves 8

quick and easy
can do ahead
can freeze

Sweet Potato Pie

- 3 large eggs
- 1 cup sugar, approximate
  dash of salt
- 1 teaspoon cinnamon
- ½ teaspoon allspice
- ¼ teaspoon freshly grated nutmeg
- 1 cup heavy cream
- 3 cups boiled sweet potatoes (3 large potatoes), mashed
- 1 unbaked 10-inch pie shell

Preheat oven to 350°.

Beat eggs well. Mix in sugar, salt and spices. Add cream and stir. Add mashed potatoes and mix well. Turn into pie shell and bake at 350° until firm to touch, about 1 hour.

Serves 8-10

quick and easy
can do ahead

Pie Crust

- 3 cups all-purpose flour
- 1 teaspoon salt
- ½ cup butter
- ½ cup vegetable shortening
- ⅓-½ cup cold water

Combine flour and salt. Cut in butter and shortening until batter is the size of small peas. Sprinkle with cold water, 1 tablespoon at a time, tossing with flour until you can squeeze a handful of dough and it sticks together.

Gather into ball and cut in half. Wrap each half in plastic wrap and form into disk. Refrigerate for at least 30 minutes or until needed. If too hard to roll out easily, let sit at room temperature until slightly softened.

Leche Flan

12	extra large or jumbo egg yolks
1	12-ounce can evaporated milk
1	8 or 12-ounce can sweetened condensed milk
2	teaspoons vanilla extract
⅔	cup dark corn syrup, not molasses
1	13-inch cake mold pan, preferably round, heart or decoratively shaped
¼	yard cheesecloth
	hot water

Preheat oven to 350°.

Stir evaporated and condensed milk into egg yolks in large glass bowl. Mix well. Add vanilla extract and mix again. Do not beat or cause bubbles. Mixture should not be at all bubbly.

Pour dark syrup to line bottom of ungreased mold so bottom is evenly coated. Pour egg mixture into mold through cheesecloth to ensure a very smooth, velvety texture.

Place mold into larger pan filled with hot water. Water level should be approximately ½ of the way up mold's sides.

Bake uncovered in 350° oven 45 minutes to 1 hour, until wooden toothpick inserted through comes out clean.

When done, take mold out of hot water bath and cool on counter or refrigerate. Never freeze. Unmold onto decorative plate. Dark syrup will now be caramelized on top of custard.

Serves at least 12

 *do ahead*

Sweet Potato Pumpkin Pudding
St. Lucia

1   18-ounce can sweet potatoes, drained
2   eggs, well beaten
1   cup canned coconut milk
1   cup canned pumpkin
½   teaspoon finely shredded orange peel
⅓   cup sugar
2   tablespoons all-purpose flour
1   teaspoon ground cinnamon
¼   teaspoon ground cloves
¼   teaspoon salt
    sweetened whipped cream
    toasted shredded coconut, optional

Preheat oven to 350°.

Mash sweet potatoes in food processor or put through a sieve. In large mixing bowl, beat eggs with coconut milk and combine with pumpkin, mashed sweet potatoes and orange peel.

In another bowl, stir together sugar, flour, cinnamon, cloves and ¼ teaspoon salt. Mix well. Combine with pumpkin mixture and spoon into 6-ounce souffle or individual custard cups. Bake in 350° oven for 50 minutes.

Serve with dollops of whipped cream and garnish with toasted coconut, if desired.

Serves 6

easy
can do ahead

Cook's Tip :

*If you do not have an
ice cream maker, pour
ice cream into shallow
metal pan and place
in freezer. Stir
occasionally until firm
and frozen. If it
freezes too hard to
stir, place in food
processor and process
until smooth.*

"Pink Champagne" Ice Cream

*Thanks to the sherry, this elegant ice cream keeps its creamy consistency
for days in the freezer.*

- 3 quarts half-and-half
- 3 scant cups sugar
- 1 cup sherry, dry or cream
- 2 drops red food coloring

Stir ingredients together until sugar dissolves and churn in ice cream
freezer. Serve immediately or save up to one week.

Serves 20

 *quick and easy
can do ahead*

Clafouti

*This wonderfully homey French dessert from the Limousin region is
traditionally prepared with cherries, but other fruits can be substituted.*

- 3 cups pitted black cherries (drained if canned)
- 1¼ cups milk
- ⅔ cup sugar, divided
- 3 eggs
- 1 tablespoon vanilla extract
- ⅛ teaspoon salt
- ⅔ cup sifted all-purpose flour
  powdered sugar in a shaker

Preheat oven to 350°.

Place in blender in order: milk, ¼ cup sugar, eggs, vanilla, salt and
flour. Blend at top speed 1 minute. (If you have no blender, work eggs
into flour with wooden spoon, gradually beat in liquids, then strain
through fine sieve.)

Pour ½-inch layer of batter in 7 to 8-cup fireproof, buttered baking
dish. Set on stove top over moderate heat for 1-2 minutes until a film
of batter has set in the bottom. Remove from heat and spread cherries
over set batter. Sprinkle with remaining ⅓ cup sugar and pour on the
rest of batter.

Place in middle of 350° oven and bake about 1 hour. Clafouti is done
when puffed and browned, but not too brown. Sprinkle with
powdered sugar just before serving.

Serves 4-6

Tres Leches

This traditional Costa Rican dessert has a wonderful consistency somewhere between custard and cake.

6	eggs, separated
1¼	cups flour
1¼	cups sugar
1	teaspoon baking powder
1	14-ounce can sweetened condensed milk, low-fat okay
1	12-ounce can evaporated milk, low-fat okay
1	cup heavy cream
1	teaspoon vanilla
¼	teaspoon almond extract

Preheat oven to 325°.

Beat egg whites until foamy. Fold in yolks. Mix together flour, sugar and baking powder and fold into eggs.

Spray 9x11-inch baking pan with vegetable oil spray and pour in egg mixture. Bake in 325° oven until browned and set, about 30 minutes. Texture will be unusual, not like typical cake.

While cake bakes, put all milks, cream and flavorings in blender and blend well. Adjust amounts to fill blender. Pour ⅔ of milk sauce over slightly warm cake. Mixture will soak through. Reserve remaining sauce.

Cut cake in squares and spoon sauce over.

Serves 15-20

*easy
can do ahead*

Cook's Tip:

This is not a recipe for dieters, but using low-fat condensed and evaporated milk might make you feel a little less guilty. You can almost always substitute them in recipes that call for condensed or evaporated milks.

Gypsy

This trifle-like dessert makes a festive finish to a holiday meal.

1   cup sugar
3   eggs
4   cups milk
   vanilla to taste

1   1-pound pound cake cut into 1-inch slices or enough
   lady fingers to line serving bowl
½   pint whipping cream
   toasted slivered almonds
   Sherry to taste

To make boiled custard, beat eggs and add sugar. Add 1 cup milk and mix. Add mixture to remaining milk in top of double boiler. Add vanilla and cook on high until water comes to boil, then cook on medium until custard begins to thicken, stirring constantly to avoid lumping or sticking. Do not allow custard to become too thick as it thickens more as it cools.

Stick almonds into pound cake slices or lady fingers. Line bottom and sides of deep glass serving or trifle bowl with cake slices or lady fingers. Sprinkle with sherry and pour on some of boiled custard. Continue layering with cake, sherry and custard.

Whip cream and use to top cake. Refrigerate overnight. Can top each piece with cherry or berry to add color if desired.

Serves 8

 *do ahead*

> "The recipe for this dessert is over 100 years old. It is commonly served in Abbeville, South Carolina, during the Thanksgiving and Christmas seasons, but delicious any time. This is a true favorite of my father."
>
> Cookie McKay,
> Woodward teacher,
> wife and mother of
> Woodward alumni

One-Step Pound Cake

2¼ cups all-purpose flour
2 cups sugar
1 cup butter
3 eggs
1 teaspoon vanilla
1 8-ounce orange yogurt, lemon yogurt, or sour cream
½ teaspoon baking soda
½ teaspoon salt
1 teaspoon grated lemon peel or ½ teaspoon lemon extract

Preheat oven to 325°.

Blend all ingredients at low speed in mixer, then beat 3 minutes at medium. Bake in greased and floured bundt pan at 325° until done, 60-70 minutes.

Serve plain or topped with fruit, ice cream or topping of your choice.

Serves 24

quick and easy
can do ahead
can freeze

Jake's Caramel Sauce

1 pound light brown sugar
1 teaspoon salt
1 cup half-and-half
½ cup butter
12 marshmallows

Mix all ingredients in top of double boiler. Stir over medium-high heat until smooth. Keep in well sealed jar. Re-warms well in microwave. Serve over pound cake or ice cream.

Krümel-Kuchen

The fruit's in the middle in this traditional German cake.

½ cup cornstarch
1½ cups plain flour
½ teaspoon baking powder
1 egg yolk
¼ cup sugar
¾ cup unsalted butter, softened
4 cups fresh sliced plums, peaches or fruit of choice
   powdered sugar

Preheat oven to 425°.

Combine cornstarch, flour and baking powder. Add sugar, egg yolk and butter. Mix on low until crumbly. Pat ¾ of dough in 9 or 10-inch springform pan. Add plums and sprinkle remaining dough on top. Bake in 425° oven 25-35 minutes. Sprinkle with powdered sugar.

Serves 6-8

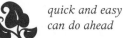

quick and easy
can do ahead

Lemon Madness Pound Cake

Cook's Tip:
Always juice fruits at room temperature. To increase amount of juice, dip fruit in hot water before squeezing, roll fruit between your palm and the counter, or place fruit in microwave 20-30 seconds.

1½ cups butter, room temperature
8 ounces cream cheese, room temperature
3 cups sugar
¼ cup fresh lemon juice
1 tablespoon grated lemon peel
1½ tablespoons vanilla extract
½ teaspoon nutmeg, preferably freshly grated
6 large eggs, room temperature
3 cups all-purpose flour
½ teaspoon salt

1¾ cups powdered sugar
3 tablespoons milk
1 tablespoon lemon juice

Preheat oven to 350°.

Cream together butter, cream cheese, and sugar until smooth, about 5 minutes. Add lemon juice and peel, vanilla, and nutmeg and beat. Beat in eggs, 2 at a time. Combine flour and salt. Stir into batter until smooth.

Grease and flour 10-inch tube pan. Pour batter in pan and bake at 350° for 1 hour and 10 minutes. Cool in pan for 15 minutes and invert onto cake plate. Re-invert cake if you want the pretty top side to show.

Combine remaining ingredients for glaze and spoon over cake while still warm. If cake is cool when glazed it will be pretty but will not absorb glaze as well. Cake stays moist up to 1 week.

Serves 12

 *can do ahead*

Lazy Daisy Oatmeal Cake

This cool-weather cake packs and travels well for tailgate parties, school lunches, and trips to visit family or friends.

1¼	cups boiling water
1	cup uncooked quick oats
½	cup softened butter
1	cup sugar
1	cup firmly packed brown sugar
1	teaspoon vanilla
2	eggs
1½	cups sifted all-purpose flour
¼	teaspoon nutmeg
1	teaspoon baking soda
½	teaspoon salt
¾	teaspoon cinnamon
½	cup melted butter
1	cup firmly packed brown sugar
3	tablespoons milk
1	cup chopped pecans
1½	cups flaked or shredded coconut

Preheat oven to 350°.

Pour boiling water over oats. Cover and let stand 20 minutes. Grease and flour 9x13-inch baking pan.

Beat butter until creamy. Gradually add sugars and beat until fluffy. Blend in vanilla and eggs. Add oat mixture. Mix well.

Sift together dry ingredients and add to creamed mixture. Mix well. Pour into prepared pan and bake in 350° oven 50-55 minutes. When finished baking, do NOT remove from pan. Make holes with fork on cake's top.

Combine remaining ingredients and spread evenly over warm cake. Run under broiler until icing becomes bubbly. Serve warm or cold, preferably after cake has rested for a day to let icing soak through the holes into the cake. If covered while still warm, cake will be moist and icing sticky. If left uncovered while cooling, icing will be stiffer and more like candy. Both ways taste good.

Serves 10-12

 *can do ahead*

Pavlova

"Our family is from New Zealand where this is the traditional dessert. While you can add any fruit you like, Kiwi and passion fruit are native to New Zealand, like the Pavlova itself."

Margaret Camac,
Woodward parent

Variation:

It would be possible to make 2 smaller Pavlovas or even several small individual ones. Adjust baking times. For 2 smaller Pavlovas, bake at 275° for 10 minutes, at 250° for 1 hour, then turn off oven and leave inside for 30 minutes.

6	egg whites
¼	teaspoon cream of tartar
	pinch salt
¾	cup sugar
¾	cup sugar mixed with 1 tablespoon cornstarch
1	teaspoon white vinegar
1	teaspoon vanilla extract
	whipped cream
	fresh fruit

Preheat oven to 275°.

Add cream of tartar and pinch of salt to egg whites and beat until very stiff. Gradually add ¾ cup sugar and beat until sugar is dissolved. Fold in remaining ¾ cup sugar mixed with cornstarch. Fold in vinegar and vanilla extract.

Empty onto 2 layers of brown paper that has been thoroughly saturated with water or on a flat cookie sheet lined with waxed paper. Shape Pavlova into large circle 3 inches deep. Bake at 275° for first 10 minutes, then 1½ hours more at 250°. Turn off oven and leave Pavlova inside with door ajar 30 minutes longer.

Invert onto a plate and gently peel off brown paper. Re-invert onto serving platter. When cool, spread with whipped cream and add fruit (cherries, sliced peaches, grapes, kiwi and/or passion fruit or whatever fruit or berry is in season). For easier slicing, place in freezer for 1-2 hours before serving.

Serves 8-10

 *can do ahead*

Schaum Torte

An Austrian classic that is somehow light and rich at the same time

12	egg whites, room temperature
2	teaspoons vanilla
1½	teaspoons vinegar
3	cups sifted sugar
3½	cups whipping cream
2½	cups crushed pineapple, drained
1	cup quartered maraschino cherries
⅓	cup rum

Preheat oven to 300°.

To room temperature egg whites, beat in vanilla and vinegar. Add sugar, 1 tablespoon at a time. Beat until very stiff and sugar dissolves.

Spread onto 3 9-inch rounds of parchment or brown paper on cookie sheets. Bake in 300° oven for 1 hour 15 minutes. Don't worry if meringues crack or break; whipped cream will cover all errors. These can be made several days ahead and stored wrapped in plastic bags at room temperature until ready to use.

Whip cream in medium large bowl. Add fruit and rum and mix gently. Spread fruit cream between layers of meringue and on top and sides.

Chill 12 hours or overnight.

Serve garnished with cherries or chocolate curls.

Serves 8-10

easy
can do partially ahead

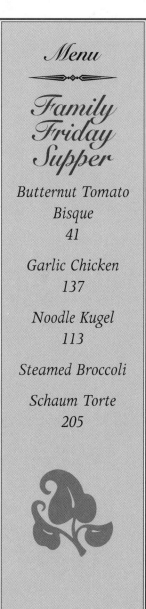

Menu

Family Friday Supper

Butternut Tomato Bisque
41

Garlic Chicken
137

Noodle Kugel
113

Steamed Broccoli

Schaum Torte
205

Espresso Shadow Cake

"My mother made three of these for my wedding reception 20 years ago. She prepared the cakes ahead, then finished them on the day of the wedding. They were the best wedding present I received. The cakes were so impressive, I had no idea how easy they were to make."

Liza Nelson Brown, Woodward parent

8 eggs
1 tablespoon plus 1 teaspoon instant coffee or espresso powder dissolved in 1 tablespoon water
1¼ cups sugar
1¼ cups all-purpose flour
1¼ teaspoons baking powder

1½ pints heavy cream
3 tablespoons confectioners' sugar
1½ tablespoon instant coffee dissolved in 1 tablespoon water
pinch of salt

2 ounces unsweetened chocolate
2 tablespoons butter
4 tablespoons sour cream
¼ teaspoon vanilla
½ cup confectioners' sugar

Preheat oven to 325°.

Separate eggs. In medium bowl, beat yolks well. Add coffee and half the sugar.

In large bowl of electric mixer, beat whites with pinch of salt until they form soft peaks. Add remaining sugar to whites, beating well. Fold yolk mixture into whites. Sift flour together with baking powder and fold into eggs, 1 tablespoon at a time. Bake in large ungreased tube pan in 325° oven for 45 minutes. Cake can be made ahead and frozen. Defrost before proceeding.

For filling, whip heavy cream. Add confectioners' sugar, coffee, and salt. For glaze, melt chocolate with butter over double boiler. Add sour cream, vanilla, and confectioners' sugar. Add more coffee if necessary to keep glaze a fairly thin consistency.

Shortly before serving, slice cake into 3 layers. Put whipped cream and some chocolate glaze between layers, then ice cake with remaining cream and drizzle chocolate glaze over. This cake tastes best the day it is completed.

Serves 16

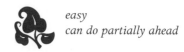
easy
can do partially ahead

Coconut White Chocolate Cake

A very grown-up cake that kids love too

- ¼ pound (¾ cup) white chocolate
- 4 eggs, separated, whites and yolks to be used
- 2 cups sugar
- 1 cup butter at room temperature
- 1 teaspoon vanilla extract
- 1 teaspoon coconut extract
- 2½ cups all-purpose flour
- 1 teaspoon baking powder
- 1 cup buttermilk

- 1½ cups granulated sugar
- 2 egg whites
- ¼ teaspoon salt
- ⅓ cup water
- ¼ teaspoon cream of tartar

- 1 teaspoon vanilla
- 3 cups freshly grated or canned coconut

Preheat oven to 350°.

Grease and flour 3 9-inch cake pans.

Melt chocolate in double boiler or microwave, stir until smooth, and cool to room temperature. Beat egg whites until stiff and place in refrigerator until needed.

Cream butter and sugar until smooth and light, 8-10 minutes. Beat in yolks 1 at a time. Add vanilla, coconut extract and melted chocolate. Combine flour and baking powder, add to butter mixture alternately with buttermilk, beginning and ending with flour. Fold in egg whites.

Pour batter into cake pans and bake at 350° for about 30 minutes. Cake is done when toothpick comes out clean from near the center. Cool in pan about 5 minutes, then turn out onto cake racks. Don't worry if cake looks slightly ragged. Frosting will cover the flaws.

Combine next 5 ingredients in top of double boiler. Because beaters need to come in contact with as much of mixture as possible, a round-bottomed metal bowl works best. Beat well. Place over pan of rapidly boiling water and beat constantly 7 minutes or until icing holds a peak. Remove from heat and add vanilla. Beat until cool and thick enough to spread. Spread icing between layers and sprinkle with coconut. Ice tops and sides and cover with coconut.

Serves 10

can do ahead

207

Lemon Cheese Filling and Frosting

2½ cups sugar
½ cup butter, softened
6 eggs
juice and grated rind of 3 lemons (about ⅔ cup juice)
pinch of salt

Place sugar and butter in heavy-bottomed saucepan. Beat eggs and add to sugar mixture. Add juice and grated rind. Add salt. Cook over low heat, stirring constantly, until mixture is almost as thick as pudding, 20-30 minutes. Set aside until completely cooled. Fill and frost cold layers of Easy Layer Cake with cooled mixture. It will remain somewhat sticky.

Cook's Tip:

For layer cake ingredients to blend properly, all ingredients should be at room temperature. To bring cold eggs to room temperature quickly, place eggs in bowl of warm water for 10 minutes.

Southern Memories Cakes

If you were raised in the South, chances are your grandmother made one, and probably both, of these cakes. Caramel Cake and Lemon Cheese Cake (no relation to cream cheese cake, this one is actually made with lemon curd) are southern classics. When people had more time to bake, these cakes turned up regularly at church suppers and Sunday dinners. If you take the time to make one of these delicious cakes, the memories will come flooding back with your first bite.

Easy Layer Cake

3 cups all-purpose flour
1½ teaspoons baking powder
½ teaspoon salt
3 sticks butter, room temperature
3 cups sugar
5 eggs, room temperature
1 cup "sweet" milk (whole milk to non-southerners)
1 teaspoon vanilla

Preheat oven to 350°.

Grease and flour three 9-inch round cake pans.

Sift flour, baking powder and salt together. Set aside.

In large bowl, use electric beater to cream butter slightly. Add sugar and cream on medium speed until mixture looks fluffy and color lightens, about 10 minutes. This step is crucial for light layers.

Add eggs one at a time, beating after each one. Add flour and milk alternately, beginning and ending with flour. Beat in vanilla.

Pour batter into cake pans and bake at 350° until layers brown and pull away from pans, 30 to 35 minutes. Cool in pan 5 minutes, then turn out and cool completely on wire racks.

Frost and fill with caramel or lemon cheese frosting.

Serves 12-14

can do ahead

Mama Grace's Caramel Cake

3 firmly packed cups light brown sugar
½ cup butter, room temperature
1 cup whipping cream
1 teaspoon vanilla
1 Easy Layer Cake, (3 layers)

Mix together brown sugar, butter and whipping cream in saucepan and bring to rolling boil. Boil 5 minutes, stirring constantly. Take pan off heat and stir in vanilla. Beat mixture with hand mixer until spreadable and heavy, about 10 minutes. Spread between cake layers and on top and sides. Don't worry if frosting runs down sides at first. Keep spreading frosting back up cake sides, and as it cools, it will stay put. Serve alone or with a scoop of vanilla ice cream on the side.

Raspberry Bars

These are addictive.

2¼ cups all-purpose flour
1 cup sugar
1 cup chopped pecans
1 cup softened butter
1 egg
1 10-ounce jar raspberry preserves

Preheat oven to 350°.

In large mixing bowl, combine flour, sugar, pecans, butter and egg. Beat at low speed, scraping bowl often until mixture is crumbly, 2-3 minutes. Reserve 1½ cups crumb mixture.

Press remaining crumb mixture on bottom of 8-inch square baking pan. Spread preserves to within ½ inch of edge. Crumble remaining mixture over preserves.

Bake in 350° oven until lightly browned, 40-50 minutes. Cool completely and cut into bars.

Makes about 30 bars

 *easy*
can do ahead

> *"Mom has always made caramel cake for our family gatherings. Of course, she's never satisfied with the way it looks, and it is always the first dessert to disappear. Now that she's getting older, we all hold our breath to see if she brings it."*
>
> Vicki Jackson,
> wife of
> Woodward President,
> Tom Jackson

> *"Christmas is a time when my mom and I make Christmas cookies. My favorites are the jelly filled. You take a ball of dough and push in a hole with your thumb, then you bake it, then when you take it out, put jelly in the hole."*
>
> Kate Carlisle,
> fourth grade
> Woodward student

Orange Almond Biscotti

This crisp, twice-baked Italian cookie is traditionally served after dinner, dipped in sweet wine; but it is equally good with an afternoon cup of coffee.

2	cups blanched almonds, coarsely chopped
3½	cups all-purpose flour
1	teaspoon baking powder
¼	teaspoon baking soda
½	cup butter, melted and cooled
2	eggs
1½	cups sugar
1	tablespoon finely chopped orange zest
1	teaspoon orange oil

Preheat oven to 350°.

Toast almonds until very light brown, 5-7 minutes.

In large bowl, mix almonds, flour, baking powder, and baking soda.

In another bowl, beat eggs, add butter, sugar, orange zest and orange oil. Beat with wire whisk until well combined. Add wet mixture to flour mixture, then mix and fold together until firm dough forms. A large spatula works best here.

Turn dough onto lightly floured surface and form into 2 logs about 14x3 inches. If dough is too soft to shape easily, knead in a little more flour. Place logs on lightly greased cookie sheet about 2 inches apart.

Bake at 350° until top is brown and firm to touch, about 30 minutes. Remove from oven and cool in pan 10 minutes. Do not turn off oven yet.

On cutting board, slice logs diagonally into ½-inch slices. Return to cookie sheet, cut side up, and bake an additional 15-20 minutes, or until cut sides are lightly browned. Cookies may be turned over after about 12 minutes to brown both sides. Cool on wire racks.

If stored in airtight container, biscotti will stay crisp for weeks.

Makes 40 cookies

 *can do ahead*

Variation:

Orange oil is what gives these biscotti an intense orange flavor. It can be found in gourmet food shops, but if you cannot find orange oil, increase the amount of zest to 2 tablespoons and add 1 teaspoon orange extract. Walnuts or pecans can be used in place of almonds.

Cook's Tip:

To make using zest easier, peel zest from orange and coarsely chop by hand, then place in blender or food processor with ½ cup sugar used in recipe. Blend or process until zest is finely minced.

Christmas Ginger Cookies

These cookies are best when soft and slightly gooey.

2	cups all-purpose flour
1	teaspoon ginger
1	teaspoon cinnamon
2	teaspoons baking soda
½	teaspoon salt
¾	cup shortening
1	cup sugar
1	egg
¼	cup molasses
½	cup sugar

Preheat oven to 350°.

Combine first 5 ingredients in small bowl.

In larger bowl, cream shortening and 1 cup sugar. Beat in egg and molasses. Stir dry ingredients into creamed mixture.

Roll into 2-inch balls and roll balls in remaining ½ cup sugar. Place 2 inches apart on ungreased cookie sheet.

Bake at 350° until lightly browned, 12-15 minutes. Do not overcook. Cookies should be soft. If they are too soft to come off the cookie sheet just out of the oven, let them sit a few minutes and try again.

Makes 5 dozen cookies

easy
can do ahead

> *"My children don't think Christmas could possibly occur without ginger cookies. They have literally come to blows over who gets the last one on the plate."*
>
> *Jan Perkins,*
> *Woodward parent*

Cook's Tip:

Bread flour should be used in this recipe to give the shortbread its characteristic crispness. All-purpose flour can be used, but the shortbread will be more tender than crisp.

Variation:

This batter can also be pressed into shortbread molds and baked according to the directions that come with the mold.

Shortbread Cookies

Because these cookies keep their shape when baked, rising very little, they are great to bake and decorate at holiday time.

1	cup butter
½	cup granulated sugar
2	cups bread flour
1	teaspoon vanilla

Preheat oven to 325°.

In food processor, cream butter and sugar. Add flour and vanilla, pulse until dough is formed. Turn dough out onto plastic wrap and form into disk. Refrigerate until firm, about 20 minutes. Roll out on well-floured board, cut into desired shapes and bake on ungreased cookie sheet at 325° for 12-15 minutes or until lightly browned around edges. Remove from pan and cool on wire racks.

(To prepare these cookies by hand, cream butter and sugar, then add vanilla. Add flour to butter mixture; the last of the flour will probably need to be added by hand. Dough should be very stiff. Knead until all ingredients are combined and form into disk. Dough made by hand may not need to be chilled. Roll out and cut as above.)

Makes 3 dozen cookies

easy
can do ahead

Czechoslovakians

So much easier than they taste, these freeze well and are perfect for holiday giving.

1	cup butter
1	cup sugar
1	egg
2	cups sifted plain flour
1	cup chopped pecans
½	12-ounce jar apricot jam or preserves
	few drops lemon juice

Preheat oven to 350°.

Cream butter and sugar. Add egg, beating well. Add flour and blend.

Grease 8x8-inch baking pan. Spread half of batter in pan. Mix preserves, nuts and lemon juice; spread over batter in pan. Cover with remaining batter; the second layer of batter may be sticky.

Bake at 350° until golden about 1 hour.

Cut into squares to serve.

Makes 25-30 squares

*easy
do ahead
can freeze*

Cook's Tip:
Slightly wet fingers will not stick to the batter and make spreading easier.

Honey Grapes

2	pounds white seedless grapes
1	cup sour cream
2	tablespoons brown sugar
2	ounces white rum
½	cup honey
	juice from 2 lemons

Mix together all ingredients except grapes. When well blended, gently stir in grapes and refrigerate at least 4 hours before serving.

Serve in glass bowls with cookies.

Serves 15

*quick and easy
do ahead*

"When I was a child, my mother would make these for company, only she would peel the grapes!"

*D.D. Cardwell,
Woodward parent*

"Southern Cracker" Toffee

	saltine crackers
1	cup packed brown sugar
1	cup butter
12	ounces chocolate chips

Preheat oven to 350°.

Line sided 11x17-inch cookie sheet with aluminum foil. Line pan with one layer of saltine crackers.

Boil 1 cup brown sugar with 1 cup butter. Pour over saltines and bake in 350° oven for 10 minutes. Remove from oven and pour chocolate chips over pan. When chocolate melts, spread over crackers. Harden in refrigerator.

Once chilled, break into pieces.

Serves 6-8

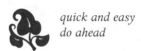

*quick and easy
do ahead*

Microwave Pecan Brittle

½	cup light corn syrup
1	cup sugar
1	cup pecan halves
1¼	teaspoons butter
1	teaspoon vanilla extract
1	teaspoon baking soda

Stir together corn syrup and sugar in 1½ quart casserole and microwave on high 4 minutes. Stir in nuts and microwave 3-5 minutes more until light brown. Add butter and vanilla. Blend well and microwave on high 1-2 minutes. Syrup will be very hot and nuts slightly browned.

Add baking soda and stir until foamy. Pour onto LARGE cookie sheet sprayed with non-stick vegetable spray. Cool at least 1 hour. Break into pieces.

Serves 16

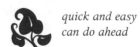

*quick and easy
can do ahead*

Chocolate
Chocolate
Chocolate

Chocolate, Chocolate, Chocolate

Regal Eagle Chocolate Cake

This is it, the favorite out of literally dozens of chocolate cakes tested.
(Hey, it's a tough job, but somebody has to do it.)

3	ounces unsweetened chocolate
2¼	cups sifted cake flour
2	teaspoons baking soda
½	teaspoon salt
½	cup butter
2¼	cups packed brown sugar
3	large eggs, room temperature
1½	teaspoons vanilla extract
1	cup sour cream
1	cup boiling water

8	ounces unsweetened chocolate
1	cup butter
2	pounds confectioners' sugar
1	cup heavy cream
4	teaspoons vanilla extract
1¼	cups coarsely chopped milk chocolate chips

Preheat oven to 350°.

Grease and flour 3 9-inch cake pans. Melt 3 ounces of chocolate in double boiler or microwave. Set aside to cool.

In medium bowl, sift together flour, soda and salt. In larger bowl, cream butter. Add brown sugar and eggs, one at a time, to butter. Beat on high speed 5 minutes. Beat in vanilla and melted chocolate. Beat in flour alternately with sour cream. Stir in boiling water and immediately pour into prepared pans.

Bake in 350° oven until center springs back when lightly touched, about 35 minutes. Cool in pans on racks 10 minutes, then invert onto racks to cool completely.

To make frosting, melt chocolate and butter in double boiler. In medium bowl, blend sugar, cream and vanilla until smooth. Add chocolate and mix on low until blended. Refrigerate 20-30 minutes.

Place 1 cake layer on dish. Spread ¼ frosting on top, sprinkle with ½ cup chocolate chips. Add second layer and repeat with frosting and chips. Add top layer and frost. Sprinkle with remaining chips.

Serves at least 10

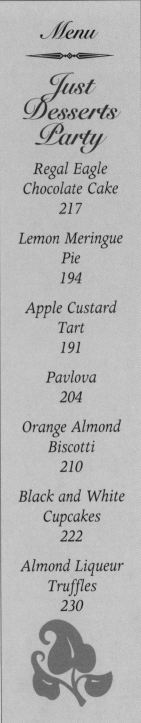

Menu

Just Desserts Party

Regal Eagle Chocolate Cake
217

Lemon Meringue Pie
194

Apple Custard Tart
191

Pavlova
204

Orange Almond Biscotti
210

Black and White Cupcakes
222

Almond Liqueur Truffles
230

Cook's Tip:

To melt chocolate in microwave instead of on top of stove,

place ¼-1 pound chopped chocolate in uncovered glass bowl and microwave on high for 1 minute. Chocolate should be soft but still hold some shape. Remove chocolate from microwave and give it a good stir. If chocolate is not completely melted, return to microwave for 10-second intervals to melt, but be careful. A few seconds too long, and you'll have burnt chocolate.

Flourless Chocolate Ring Cake

Elegant and splashy, yet easy to prepare

    8   ounces chopped semi-sweet chocolate
    1   cup butter, softened
    4   eggs
    1   cup sugar
    6   tablespoons cornstarch
    2   tablespoons raspberry liqueur

    1   cup Mandarin orange sections
    1   cup fresh raspberries (frozen okay, thawed)
    1   cup whipped cream

Preheat oven to 350°.

Coat 1¼-quart ring mold with vegetable oil cooking spray and dust with flour, knocking out excess.

Melt chocolate in double boiler. In large bowl, cream butter with electric mixer. Add chocolate and blend well.

In another bowl, whisk eggs with sugar until well combined. Add egg mixture to chocolate and beat thoroughly. Sift cornstarch over batter and stir in. Add raspberry liqueur, stirring until batter is well mixed.

Spoon batter into prepared ring mold. Place mold in baking pan. Add enough hot water to pan to reach half way up the side of the mold. Bake on middle shelf of 350° oven until tester comes out clean, 1 hour to 1 hour and 10 minutes.

Cool cake completely in mold, then lift mold off cake. Can prepare ahead and keep up to 1 day at room temperature.

When ready to serve, combine oranges and berries and fold into whipping cream. Mound fruit and cream mixture in center of chocolate ring and serve.

Serves 8-10

 *can do ahead*

Chocolate Pound Cake

A dense, moist pound cake

- 3 cups all-purpose flour
- 3 cups sugar
- 7 tablespoons cocoa
- 1 cup whole milk
- 1 teaspoon vanilla
- 1 pound melted butter
- 5 eggs

Preheat oven to 325°.

In large bowl, combine flour, sugar and cocoa. Blend. Add milk and vanilla to flour mixture, then add melted butter.

Add eggs, one at a time, mixing well after each addition.

Grease and flour bundt pan or loaf pan. Pour batter into pan and bake in 325° oven for 1½ hours.

To serve cut into small pieces. Cake is quite rich.

Serves 10-12

easy
can do ahead

Chocolate Chip Butterscotch Squares

- 2 firmly packed cups light or dark brown sugar
- ⅔ cup melted butter
- 3 eggs
- 2½ cups self-rising flour
- 1 teaspoon vanilla
- 6 ounces semi-sweet chocolate chips
- 1 cup pecan pieces, optional

Preheat oven to 350°.

With mixer, blend brown sugar and melted butter until smooth. Add eggs one at a time, slowly blending after each. Spoon in flour, about ¾ cup at a time, blending after each addition until well mixed. Add vanilla. Stir in chocolate chips and pecans.

Lightly grease 13x9x2-inch pan. Pour batter in pan and bake in 350° oven for 30 minutes. Cool and cut into desired square size.

Makes about 3 dozen

quick and easy
can do ahead
can freeze

Variation:

To dress these up, place 2 ounces of semi-sweet chocolate in zip-lock bag and microwave to melt, checking every 30 seconds. When completely melted, snip off corner of bag and squeeze chocolate out in zig-zag pattern over top of uncut cookie. Allow to harden before cutting into squares.

You could also use mint or raspberry chocolate chips for a twist.

Flat Black Cake

Kids always go for this sheet cake made with cocoa.

    2   cups all-purpose flour
    2   cups sugar
    1   cup butter
    4   tablespoons cocoa
    1   cup water
    2   eggs
    ½   cup buttermilk
    1   teaspoon baking soda

    ¾   cup butter
    4   tablespoons cocoa
  6-8   tablespoons milk (enough for good spreading
        consistency)
    1½ boxes powdered sugar
    1   teaspoon vanilla
    1   cup chopped pecans, optional

Preheat oven to 400°.

In large mixing bowl, sift together flour and sugar.

In saucepan, mix together butter, cocoa and water. Heat through for 1 minute or until butter melts.

Add chocolate mixture to flour mixture. Whisk in eggs, buttermilk and baking soda. Pour into lightly greased 9x13-inch or 10x14-inch pan and bake at 400° for 20 minutes.

While cake is baking, prepare icing. In saucepan, mix butter, cocoa and milk. Bring to simmer, then remove from heat. Beat in sugar and vanilla, plus chopped pecans if desired.

Pour icing over hot cake as soon as you remove cake from oven.

Serves 24

 easy
can do ahead

Chocolate Cappuccino Cheesecake

For those times you really want to impress your guests, this will do it.

- 1½ cups chocolate sandwich cookie crumbs, about 20 cookies
- ¼ cup melted butter
- 3 8-ounce packages cream cheese
- ¾ cup sugar
- 3 eggs
- ½ cup strong, brewed coffee
- 12 ounces semi-sweet or bittersweet chocolate, melted
- 2 teaspoons vanilla
- 8 ounces (1 cup) sour cream

Preheat oven to 350°.

Mix cookie crumbs with butter and press into bottom of buttered 10x2-inch round cake pan.

Beat cream cheese and sugar until completely combined, then add eggs 1 at a time, beating well after each addition. Add coffee and beat until combined. Add chocolate and vanilla and beat again. Add sour cream and beat on medium speed until batter is all one color.

Pour batter into cookie crust. Place pan in large roasting pan. Pour very hot, but not boiling, water around cheesecake pan to come about 1-inch up its side. Bake in 350° oven 45 minutes, then turn oven off and leave cheesecake in oven 1 more hour.

Cool cheesecake in pan until room temperature, then refrigerate until completely chilled, preferably overnight.

To unmold, cover flat plate, at least 10 inches in diameter, with plastic wrap. Place cheesecake pan on heated burner and move in circle about 10 seconds, then run thin-bladed knife around sides to release. Place plate on top and invert. If cake doesn't come out immediately, run knife around sides again and heat a few seconds longer.

Re-invert cake onto serving platter. Just before serving, decorate with whipped cream, chocolate curls and chocolate coffee beans.

Makes 16 slices

 *do ahead*

Cook's Tip:
Cheesecake baked in a waterbath remains creamy all the way to the edge. Buttering the edge of the pan prevents the cheesecake from cracking.

Cook's Tip:
To make cookie crumbs, place cookies in large zip-lock bag and beat with rolling pin, or use a food processor.

Black and White Cupcakes

These are wonderful for kids, but sophisticated adults have also been known to hoard them for the little surprise inside.

8	ounces cream cheese, room temperature
1	egg, beaten
⅓	cup sugar
¼	teaspoon salt
6	ounces chocolate chips
1½	cups flour
1	cup sugar
¼	cup cocoa
1	teaspoon baking soda
½	teaspoon salt
1	cup water
⅓	cup oil
1	tablespoon vinegar
1	teaspoon vanilla

Preheat oven to 350°.

Line mini-muffin tins with paper liners.

Mix first 5 ingredients for filling and set aside.

Mix remaining ingredients and fill mini-cupcake papers ¾ full. Add 1 teaspoon filling mixture to each. Bake 30 minutes.

Best served frozen.

Makes about 3 dozen

quick and easy
can do ahead
can freeze

Chocolate Bread Pudding

1   pound challah or egg bread loaf
2   cups whole milk
2   cups heavy cream
1   cup sugar
8   eggs
1   tablespoon vanilla
10 ounces coarsely chopped semi-sweet or
    bittersweet chocolate
¼   cup rum, optional

Preheat oven to 350°.

Cut bread into 1-inch cubes and place in a large buttered casserole dish (approximately 9x13-inches). Set aside.

In heavy-bottomed saucepan, heat cream and milk until just warm. Whisk eggs with sugar and vanilla and add to cream. Melt chocolate in double boiler or microwave. Gradually whisk chocolate into egg-cream mixture. Add rum if desired.

Pour chocolate custard over bread and let soak at least 45 minutes, pushing bread down occasionally.

Place pudding in shallow pan of hot, but not boiling, water (bain marie) and bake for 1 hour or until knife inserted in center comes out clean.

Serve warm with whipped cream or simply with heavy cream poured over top.

Serves 8-10

"A few years ago I was obsessed with chocolate. Chocolate this, chocolate that. Everything I ate was chocolate. One day my parents had had enough. 'Okay,' they said while I wasn't listening. 'We'll buy him so much chocolate that he won't want to see it ever again.' They gave me the chocolate. I was amazed. It was more chocolate than I had ever seen. So I started eating. I ate and ate and ate until my parents decided it wasn't working and took away the rest. And up to this day, I have been, and always shall be, obsessed with chocolate."

Steven Kennedy,
seventh grade
Woodward student

Double Chocolate Brownies

1¼ cups flour
¼ teaspoon baking soda
⅛ teaspoon baking powder
⅛ teaspoon salt
14 ounces chopped semi-sweet chocolate
1 cup sugar
9 tablespoons butter
¼ cup light corn syrup
¼ cup water
3 eggs
1 tablespoon vanilla
1 10-ounce bag semi-sweet chocolate chunks or
    2½ cups chopped semi-sweet squares

Preheat oven to 325°.

Line 9x13-inch baking pan with foil, spray with cooking oil.

In medium bowl, stir together flour, baking soda, baking powder and salt. Set aside.

Place 14 ounces of chocolate in large bowl.

In saucepan, melt butter, sugar, corn syrup and water. Cook until mixture begins to boil, then pour over chocolate to melt. Whisk until smooth. Add eggs, vanilla and flour mixture. Add ½ bag of chocolate chunks. Pour into pan, then scatter rest of chunks over batter. Bake 40-50 minutes at 325°.

Let cool overnight or in refrigerator.

Makes 2 dozen

easy
do ahead
can freeze

The Best Chocolate Chip Cookies

1	cup butter
1	cup sugar
1	cup brown sugar
2	eggs
1	teaspoon vanilla
2	cups flour
2½	cups oatmeal (measure, then blend to powder)
½	teaspoon salt
1	tablespoon baking powder
1	tablespoon baking soda
12	ounces semi-sweet chocolate chips
4	ounces chocolate bar, grated
1½	cups chopped nuts

Preheat oven to 375°.

In large bowl, cream butter and sugars. Add eggs and vanilla. Mix well.

In another bowl mix flour, oatmeal, salt, baking powder and baking soda. Add to creamed mixture. Stir in chocolate bar, chips and nuts. Roll into balls.

Place 2 inches apart on baking sheet and bake 10 minutes in 375° oven.

Makes 5-6 dozen

easy
can do ahead

Cook's Tip:
Oatmeal takes on a nice nutty flavor when toasted. Before using in a recipe, spread dry oatmeal out on a cookie sheet and place in 350° oven for 8-10 minutes or until light brown. Cool and use as directed.

Coffee Liqueur Chocolate Sauce

1 cup half-and-half
6 ounces semi-sweet chocolate chips
1 tablespoon coffee liqueur

Bring half-and-half to boil, add chocolate and remove from heat. Stir until melted. Cool 10 minutes and add coffee liqueur.

Brownie Pie à la Mode

2 eggs
1 cup sugar
½ cup softened butter
½ cup flour
4 tablespoons cocoa powder
1 teaspoon vanilla extract
pinch salt
½ cup chopped pecans

Preheat oven to 350°.

With electric mixer beat together all pie ingredients except pecans 5 minutes. Fold in nuts. Pour into greased 8-inch pie plate. Bake at 325° for 30 minutes.

Serve pie warm with ice cream and chocolate sauce.

Serves 6

*easy
can do ahead*

Chocolate Macadamia Nut Pie

Can a pie get much richer?

- ½ cup melted butter
- 1 cup semi-sweet chocolate chips
- ½ cup plain flour
- ½ cup white sugar
- ½ cup packed brown sugar
- 2 eggs, beaten
- 1 teaspoon vanilla
- ½ cup milk chocolate chips
- ½ cup white chocolate chips
- 1 cup coarsely chopped macadamia nuts
- 1 9-10 inch unbaked pie shell

Preheat oven to 350°.

In large bowl, combine slightly warm melted butter with semi-sweet chips. Chips will partially melt.

In separate bowl, mix flour and sugars, then add to chocolate/butter mixture along with 2 beaten eggs and vanilla. Stir until well combined. Add milk chocolate chips, white chocolate chips and macadamia nuts. Stir and pour into pie shell.

Bake at 350° until top is brown and crust appears baked, 45-50 minutes. Cool on rack.

Serve at room temperature or chilled.

Serves 8

*do ahead
can freeze*

Cook's Tip:

To freeze Chocolate Macadamia Nut Pie, overwrap with aluminum foil and place in a large freezer bag.

Variations:

If you prefer a less sweet, more fudgy pie, use 1½ cups semi-sweet chocolate chips and eliminate the white chocolate. Walnuts or pecans will work in place of macadamia nuts, or try a combination of all three.

Chocolate Meringue Pie

This recipe is for two pies because one is never enough.

2	cups sugar
3	rounded tablespoons flour
3	rounded tablespoons cocoa
4	egg yolks, beaten
2⅓	cups milk
1	teaspoon vanilla
3	tablespoons butter
2	9 or 10-inch precooked pie shells
4	egg whites
¼	teaspoon cream of tartar
½	cup sugar

Preheat oven to 375°.

In 2-quart sauce pan, mix sugar, flour, and cocoa. Add beaten egg yolks, milk and vanilla. Mix until blended. Add butter. Place pan over medium heat and stir constantly until thick, 10-12 minutes after it begins to boil.

Pour into cooled pie shells. You can make ahead to this point, in which case refrigerate filled pie shells until ready to use.

To make meringue, beat egg whites and cream of tartar until fluffy. Gradually add sugar and beat until stiff. Spoon over filling and bake at 375° for 10-12 minutes or until top is lightly browned.

Serves 8 per pie

 can partially do ahead

Chocolate Pecan Pie

1 cup packed dark brown sugar
¾ cup light corn syrup
6 tablespoons butter, cut in pieces
4 ounces semi-sweet or bittersweet chocolate, coarsely chopped
3 eggs
½ teaspoon salt
1 tablespoon vanilla extract
2 cups pecans, toasted and chopped
1 9-inch pie crust, unbaked (page 195)

Preheat oven to 350°.

Combine brown sugar and corn syrup in saucepan, place over medium heat and bring to boil. Remove from heat and add butter and chocolate. Stir until chocolate melts.

In small bowl, whisk eggs with salt and vanilla, then whisk into chocolate mixture. Stir in toasted pecans and pour into prepared crust.

Bake in 350° oven for 45 minutes or until crust is browned and filling is set and puffed. Cool pie on rack.

Serve warm or at room temperature, alone or with sweetened whipped cream.

Serves 8

 easy

> ## Cook's Tip:
>
> Brown sugar is simply white sugar with molasses added to it. If you find yourself without the brown sugar needed for a recipe, you can easily make your own. For one cup of light brown sugar, combine one cup of white sugar and ¼ cup of unsulfured light molasses. For one cup of dark brown sugar, combine one cup of white sugar and ½ cup of unsulfured light molasses. When a recipe calls for brown sugar, use light brown sugar unless otherwise specified.

Almond Liqueur Truffles

We have made these with almond liqueur but you may use any flavored liqueur.

Cook's Tip:
Temperature is key to candy making. If mixture gets too thick, either put it back on heat or remove and stir a minute. Do not let any water splash into the pan.

12	ounces semi-sweet chocolate
½	cup butter
2	egg yolks
½	cup whipping cream
¼	cup almond liqueur
18	ounces (3 cups) semi-sweet chocolate
3	tablespoons shortening

Melt chocolate in double boiler. Add butter 1 tablespoon at a time. You may need to move pan off and on heat to maintain creamy consistency.

Beat egg yolks. Add spoonful of warm chocolate mixture to eggs, then pour eggs into chocolate, stirring constantly. Add cream and liqueur and cook about 1 minute until creamy.

Remove from heat and store in freezer overnight.

Roll cold chocolate into small balls and return to freezer until firm again, about 1 hour.

Meanwhile melt 18 ounces of chocolate with shortening in double boiler over low heat just until creamy. Remove from heat. With toothpick dip chocolate balls in coating. Place on waxed paper and store in refrigerator.

Makes 3 dozen

 *do ahead*

Breakfasts
and
Breads

Breakfasts and Breads

Pineapple Raspberry Breakfast Parfait

So pretty and cool on a hot summer morning

  2 cups chopped fresh pineapple
  1 cup raspberries, fresh or frozen (and thawed)
  1 cup low-fat vanilla yogurt
  2 firm, medium bananas, peeled and sliced
 ⅓ cup chopped dates
 ¼ cup sliced toasted almonds

     fresh mint

Layer pineapple, raspberries, yogurt, banana slices and dates in
6 individual serving bowls, preferably glass. Sprinkle with toasted
almonds and mint.

Serves 6

quick and easy

> *"My favorite food is pineapple because it is gushy. I love fruit and sometimes it squirts in my face and I get all wet."*
>
> *Rochelle Morgan–Verdin,*
> *third grade*
> *Woodward student*

Thick Slicer French Toast

A definite kid pleaser

  1 loaf egg bread or challah, cut into thick slices
  3 eggs, beaten
 ⅓ cup milk or cream
 ¼ teaspoon nutmeg
 ¼ teaspoon cinnamon
 ½ teaspoon vanilla
     dash salt
  4 tablespoons butter

     brown sugar
     several limes, cut into fourths

Mix milk and eggs. Add nutmeg, cinnamon and vanilla. Dip bread
into mixture.

Melt 2 tablespoons butter in large skillet, cook bread slices on one side,
re-butter pan if needed and cook on second side until nicely browned
and cooked through.

Sprinkle with brown sugar, then squeeze lime juice on top. Amount
can vary according to degree of tartness desired.

Serves 6 or more

quick and easy

Cornmeal Porridge

Eating this porridge on a cold winter morning, you may feel as cosy as Goldilocks visiting the three bears.

- 1 cup cornmeal
- 4 cups milk
- ¼ scant teaspoon nutmeg
- ½ scant teaspoon vanilla
- ¼ teaspoon ground cinnamon
- 2 tablespoons sugar

  brown sugar
  butter or milk

Pour milk into medium saucepan, add cornmeal and mix well to remove all lumps.

Bring to boil stirring constantly. Immediately lower heat and stir in nutmeg, vanilla, cinnamon and sugar to taste. Simmer 10 minutes. Add more milk if porridge gets too thick.

Serve in bowls and sprinkle with brown sugar. Dot with a little butter or pour on a little extra milk.

Serves 6

> "When I was growing up in Jamaica, my mother always said, 'Use the side of a spoon when drinking soup, but the tip of the spoon for porridge.' Cornmeal was the popular choice for porridge although people also used oatmeal or grated green banana."
>
> *Lineve Lewis,*
> *Woodward parent*

Matzoh Brie

- 4 matzohs, broken up
- 2 whole eggs, beaten
- 1 teaspoon salt
- 1-2 teaspoons butter or oil

Soak matzohs in hot water 15 minutes. Squeeze out and add eggs and salt.

Lightly grease skillet with butter or oil. Drop mixture by spoonful into skillet and brown on each side.

Serve with sugar and sour cream or syrup.

Serves 4

 easy

Spinach and Italian Sausage Braid

- 1 pound loaf frozen bread dough
- 1 pound fresh Italian sausage, half hot, half mild
- 1 garlic clove, crushed
- 1 package frozen chopped spinach, thawed and all liquid squeezed out
- 1½ cups shredded sharp cheddar cheese
- 1½ cups shredded mozzarella cheese
- 1 egg, for glaze

Oil long cookie sheet. Rub oil by hand all over frozen bread dough. Place on cookie sheet, cover loosely with plastic wrap, then cover loosely with kitchen towel. Let rise 12 hours in draft-free area (can be done in cold oven over night).

Remove sausage from casing, break up, and brown in skillet with garlic until cooked through. Drain. Add spinach to sausage and combine. Set aside. (Recipe can be done ahead up to this point. Refrigerate mixture. When ready to use, warm slightly before proceeding.)

Preheat oven to 350°.

Uncover bread dough. With well-oiled hands, flatten dough into 8x14-inch rectangle on cookie sheet. Mound sausage down middle of dough, top with mozzarella, then cheddar. You will have a large mound.

Cut 7 diagonal slits down each side of dough almost up to sausage. Pull each strip of bread dough up and over sausage and cheese at angle to resemble braid. Tuck end pieces under loaf. Brush with beaten egg.

Bake at 350° until well browned, about 30 minutes. Braid will keep refrigerated 1 day. Warm, loosely covered with aluminum, at 350° until warmed through, about 25 minutes

Serves 12

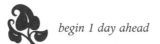 *begin 1 day ahead*

> **Cook's Tip:**
> *If braiding sounds too complicated, simply bring the two sides of dough up over sausage and pinch to close. Turn loaf over and cut 7 diagonal slits across top.*

Cook's Tip:

While any sausage will work, a mix of spicy and mild, loose and link, cut into chunks, gives the strata a memorable texture and flavor.

Cheese and Sausage Strata

1   pound sausage, browned and drained

6   eggs, beaten
2   cups milk
1   teaspoon dry mustard
     salt and pepper to taste
6   slices bread, broken into pieces

1½ cups cheddar cheese, grated
¼   cup sliced mushrooms
     paprika to taste

Beat together eggs, milk, dry mustard, salt and pepper. Add bread and stir to soften. Stir in cheese, browned sausage, and mushrooms.

Pour into greased 9x13-inch or 8x12-inch glass baking dish. Sprinkle with paprika for color. Refrigerate overnight.

In morning preheat oven to 350°, then bake 40-45 minutes.

Serve hot.

Serves 6-8

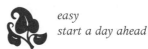

easy
start a day ahead

Eggs Royale

2   cups herb flavored croutons
1   cup shredded cheddar cheese
4   eggs, slightly beaten
2   cups milk
½   teaspoon salt
½   teaspoon dry mustard
⅛   teaspoon onion powder
½   teaspoon pepper
10 slices cooked bacon

Preheat oven to 325°.

Combine croutons and cheese and put in bottom of greased 2- quart casserole dish. Mix other ingredients, except bacon, until well blended. Pour over croutons and cheese.

Crumble bacon on top. Bake in 325° oven for 55-60 minutes.

Serves 4

easy

California Tomato Tarragon Tart

A flavorful alternative to quiche

1	uncooked pie crust (page 195)
2	tablespoons grated Parmesan cheese
¼	cup grated Parmesan cheese
4	ounces fresh chevre (goat cheese)
8	ounces cream cheese, softened
2-3	tablespoons fresh chopped tarragon
2	large tomatoes, sliced
	fresh ground black pepper to taste

Preheat oven to 350°.

Line 10-inch tart pan with pie crust. Sprinkle with 2 tablespoons Parmesan cheese.

Mix together remaining Parmesan, chevre and cream cheeses.

Add tarragon and mix. Spread in pan over crust. Top with tomato slices in layers. Sprinkle with fresh ground pepper.

Bake in 350° oven for 25 minutes. Cool tart to room temperature.

Cut into serving pieces. Delicious at room temperature or cold. It will keep refrigerated for several days, although some of the original zest gets lost.

Serves 12

easy
can do ahead

Variation:
If you can't find fresh tarragon, fresh basil also tastes wonderful in this recipe.

Lemon Blueberry Bread

¼	cup plus 2 tablespoons butter, softened
1	cup sugar
2	eggs
1½	cups plain flour
1	teaspoon baking powder
	pinch of salt
½	cup milk
2	teaspoons lemon rind, grated
1	cup fresh blueberries
⅓	cup sugar
3	tablespoons lemon juice

Preheat oven to 350°.

Cream butter. Gradually add 1 cup sugar until blended. Add eggs, one by one, beating well after each.

Combine flour, baking powder, and salt. Alternately add flour mixture and milk to creamed mixture, beginning and ending with flour mixture. Stir in lemon rind, then fold in blueberries.

Pour batter into greased 9½x4½x3-inch loaf pan or bundt pan. Bake at 350° until straw comes out clean, about 55 minutes.

To make topping, combine ⅓ cup sugar and 3 tablespoons lemon juice in small sauce pan and heat until sugar dissolves.

As soon as bread comes out of oven, puncture top all over with toothpicks. Pour lemon mixture over warm bread. Cool in pan 30 minutes.

Serves 8-10

*do ahead
can freeze*

Danish Kringle

½   cup butter
1   cup all-purpose flour
1-2 tablespoons water

1   cup water
½   cup butter
1   cup all-purpose flour
3   eggs
1   teaspoon vanilla extract

2   tablespoons butter, softened
1   cup confectioners' sugar
    pinch of salt
½   teaspoon vanilla
1½-2 tablespoons cream or milk

Preheat oven to 400°.

Cut ½ cup butter into 1 cup flour using pastry blender or 2 knives. Sprinkle with water and toss until dough begins to form. Press together into ball. Divide dough in half and roll each half with hands to make cigar shaped roll. Place dough "cigars" on ungreased cookie sheet and with fingertip push and shape dough into 2 11x3-inch rectangles. Set aside.

Bring 1 cup water and ½ cup butter to boil in sauce pan. Remove from heat and stir in 1 cup flour all at once. Beat eggs 1 at a time into mixture until mixture is smooth and shiny and pulls away from sides of bowl. Stir in vanilla. Spread mixture on dough strips and bake 30-35 minutes at 400°. Remove from oven and cool.

Cream 1 cup confectioners' sugar with 2 tablespoons softened butter, then add salt and vanilla. Gradually add milk as needed. You want to be able to drizzle icing over kringles.

Serves 6-8

 *can do ahead*

Variation:
Consider adding strawberry, apricot, or raspberry jam to the kringle. Spread jam over kringle while it is still warm after baking. Then allow kringle to cool and jam to set up before adding frosting.

Anise Kuchen

This sweet yeast bread combines the flavors of anise with orange and lemon.

1¼	cups milk
1	package yeast
¼	cup water
1	cup butter
½	cup sugar
1	teaspoon grated fresh orange rind
1	teaspoon grated fresh lemon rind
1	teaspoon salt
¼	teaspoon mace
¼	teaspoon nutmeg
1	tablespoon anise seed
3	eggs
6	cups flour

Scald 1¼ cups milk. Let cool.

Dissolve 1 package of yeast in ¼ cup water and set aside.

Melt butter in small sauce pan. Gradually add sugar.

In large bowl, combine butter, grated orange and lemon rind, salt, mace, nutmeg and anise seed. Mix in eggs, one at a time. Add yeast and cooled milk. Mix in 4 cups of flour, then 2 more cups, ½ cup at a time.

Turn out on a floured board, cover and let rise 10 minutes.

Knead, then place in a greased bowl, cover, let rise until double, about 1 hour. Punch down.

Shape into two or three very tight, round loaves. Grease dough and place on greased cookie sheet. Let rise until double, about 1 hour.

Preheat oven to 350°. When loaves have doubled, bake for 45 minutes. Place on low rack for first 20 minutes, then move to center rack to complete baking.

Makes 2 loaves

can do ahead
can freeze

Cranberry Coffee Cake with Almond Glaze

½   cup butter
1   cup sugar
2   eggs
2   cups all-purpose flour
1   teaspoon baking powder
1   teaspoon baking soda
½   teaspoon salt
1   cup sour cream
1   teaspoon almond extract
1   16-ounce can whole berry cranberry sauce
½   cup chopped pecans

Preheat oven to 350°.

In large bowl, cream butter and sugar with electric mixer until light and fluffy. Add eggs and beat well.

In another bowl, sift together dry ingredients. Add to creamed mixture alternately with sour cream, beating well after each addition. Stir in almond extract.

Spoon ⅓ of batter in greased and floured 10-inch tube pan. Spread ⅓ of cranberry sauce over batter. Repeat layers two more times, ending with cranberry sauce. Sprinkle with pecans.

Bake in 350° oven for 1 hour or until cake tests done. Cool in pan on rack for 10 minutes, then remove from pan and drizzle top with almond glaze.

Serves 8

 easy

Almond Glaze

¾   cup powdered sugar
1   tablespoon water
½   teaspoon almond extract

Mix sugar, water and almond extract together just before using.

Butterscotch Pumpkin Muffins

These are good warm or cold, and kids love them.

1¾	cups flour
½	cup packed brown sugar
½	cup sugar
½	teaspoon ginger
½	teaspoon mace
1	tablespoon cinnamon
¼	teaspoon ground cloves
1	teaspoon baking soda
¼	teaspoon baking powder
2	large eggs
1	cup canned pumpkin
1	stick melted butter
1	cup butterscotch chips

Preheat oven to 350°.

In large bowl mix all dry ingredients well. Make a well in dry ingredients.

In small bowl mix eggs, pumpkin and butter. Stir in chips. Pour into well of dry ingredients. Fold until just moistened. Do not overmix.

Pour into greased muffin tins and bake 20-25 minutes in 350° oven.

Makes 18 large or 36 small muffins

easy
can do ahead
can freeze

"These are on our table for every holiday breakfast and even Thanksgiving dinner. They have even been a big hit at cocktail parties."

Jane Van Epps,
Woodward parent

Cook's Tip:

Adjust your cooking time depending on the size of your muffin tins. A smaller muffin requires less time to bake.

Grandma Astrid's Swedish Coffee Cake

5½ cups bread flour
¼ cup sugar
1 teaspoon salt
1 teaspoon lemon peel or 2 teaspoons cardamom
2 packages active dry yeast
1 cup milk
½ cup water
1 cup butter
2 eggs, lightly beaten
1 12½-ounce can almond filling

2 cups confectioners' sugar
1 tablespoon milk or more as needed

maraschino cherries
nuts

Preheat oven to 375°.

In large bowl, thoroughly mix flour, sugar, salt, lemon peel or cardamom, and undissolved yeast. Combine milk, water and butter in saucepan. Heat over low heat until liquids are very warm, but butter does not need to melt. Gradually add along with eggs to dry ingredients and beat 2 minutes on medium speed of electric mixer, scraping bowl occasionally. Stir in enough additional flour to make a stiff dough. Cover bowl with plastic wrap and then a towel. Set aside 20 minutes to 1 hour.

Turn dough onto floured board and knead a few times until smooth. Divide in half. Roll each half into 14x10-inch rectangle. Spread each with almond filling. Roll up as for jelly roll, pinching seam to seal.

Place on ungreased baking sheet. Cut diagonal slits about 1 inch apart, starting from top surface of roll and cutting about ⅔ of way through. Pull every other cut piece to left, gently pushing remaining pieces to right to form zigzag pattern. Cover loosely with waxed paper. Refrigerate 2-24 hours or let rise at room temperature 1 hour.

Bake in 375° oven 25-30 minutes. Remove from baking sheet and cool on wire racks. Meanwhile, combine 2 cups of confectioners' sugar with enough milk to give spreading consistency. Frost cooled cake with frosting and decorate with cherries and nuts.

Serves 16

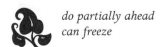

*do partially ahead
can freeze*

Menu

Mid-Morning Coffee Break

Grandma Astrid's
Swedish
Coffee Cake
243

Cinnamon Rolls
244

Danish Kringle
239

Spinach and
Italian Sausage
Braid
235

Honey Grapes
213

Cinnamon Rolls

Grandma Astrid's Swedish Coffee Cake recipe, with small changes, can produce delicious cinnamon rolls.

5½	cups bread flour
¼	cup sugar
1	teaspoon salt
2	packages active dry yeast
1	cup milk
½	cup water
1	cup butter
2	eggs, lightly beaten
12	tablespoons butter, softened
2	cups light brown sugar
2	teaspoons cinnamon
2	cups confectioners' sugar
2	tablespoons melted butter
1	tablespoon milk or more as needed

Prepare dough as in coffee cake recipe, omitting lemon peel or cardamom, and roll out 2 rectangles as for coffee cake. On each rectangle, instead of almond paste, spread 6 tablespoons softened butter. Combine brown sugar with cinnamon and sprinkle evenly over butter. Beginning on 14-inch side, roll up each rectangle and pinch to seal. Turn sealed side down and cut into 1-inch slices. Place rolls about 1 inch apart in four well-buttered 9-inch cake pans, 7 rolls per pan.

At this point pans can be covered, first with plastic wrap, then with aluminum foil, and refrigerated overnight. Allow to come to room temperature about 1 hour before baking. If not refrigerating, cover pans with plastic wrap and allow dough to rise until doubled in bulk, 1½ to 2 hours before proceeding.

Remove cover and bake in preheated 350° oven 25-30 minutes or until brown on top.

Cool rolls in pan for 10 minutes while preparing glaze. For glaze, combine 2 cups powdered sugar with 2 tablespoons melted butter, then add milk 1 tablespoon at a time until desired consistency is reached. Drizzle glaze over rolls and serve warm or at room temperature.

Makes 28 rolls

do partially ahead

Mrs. Geary's Irish Soda Bread

4	cups all-purpose flour
1	cup sugar
4	teaspoons baking powder
1	teaspoon salt
2	teaspoons caraway seed, optional
1	cup raisins
1	cup currants
4	tablespoons shortening
2-3	eggs
1¾	cups milk or enough to make soft dough

Preheat oven to 350°.

Sift flour, sugar, baking powder and salt into large bowl. Add caraway seed if desired; mix. Add raisins and currants; mix.

Cut in shortening. Beat eggs well. Add milk to them, then add to dry ingredients; use a little more milk if necessary.

Knead gently. Slightly flour top. Pat with a little milk and sprinkle on a little sugar.

Place in large spider pan or two small pans and bake in 350° oven for 1 hour.

Serves 6-8

can do ahead
can freeze

"I got this recipe from my friend Eileen whose mother came over on the boat from Ireland."
Christina O'Hara Brennan, Woodward parent

Rustic Walnut Wheat Bread

This bread makes wonderful sandwiches.

3 cups warm water
1 package dry yeast (1 scant tablespoon)
1 cup cracked wheat
3 cups whole wheat flour
1 tablespoon salt
3 cups bread flour
3 cups walnuts, toasted for 10 minutes and coarsely chopped

Place warm water in large bowl, sprinkle yeast over and let sit until dissolved, about 10 minutes. Add cracked wheat and 3 cups whole wheat flour. Stir vigorously 100 strokes to develop gluten; it will be the consistency of thick pancake batter. Cover well with plastic wrap and let sit for 30 minutes to 2 hours; the longer time helps develop flavor.

Stir down batter and add salt. Add bread flour one cup at a time, stirring after each cup is added until dough is too thick to stir. Turn out onto well-floured board and knead in enough remaining flour to form smooth, elastic dough.

Flatten dough and spread 1 cup of walnuts on top. Knead in. Repeat with 2 remaining cups of nuts. Knead until walnuts are evenly distributed in dough. Form dough into ball and place in large, well-oiled bowl, turning to coat dough with oil. Let rise 1-2 hours.

Punch down dough and form into 2 loaves. Place them in greased bread pans, cover loosely with plastic wrap and allow them to rise 1 hour or until doubled in size.

Place dough in preheated 375° oven and bake 30-35 minutes or until loaves are well browned and sound hollow when tapped on their bottoms. (If loaves seem under-cooked when removed from pan, return them to oven without pans, directly on oven rack, to help brown bottoms.)

Remove bread from pans and place on wire rack until cool. This bread will keep at room temperature for 2-3 days, or can be frozen whole or sliced. If frozen sliced, remove slices as needed and pop, frozen, into toaster.

Makes 2 loaves

can do ahead
can freeze

Southern Buttermilk Cornbread

Traditional southern cornbreads contain neither flour nor sugar.

Menu

Snowed-In Breakfast

Cornmeal Porridge
234

Cheese and
Sausage Strata
236

Mrs. Geary's
Irish Soda Bread
245

Winter Fruit
Compote
180

4	tablespoons butter
2	cups cornmeal
½	teaspoon baking powder
1	teaspoon baking soda
1	teaspoon salt
2	cups buttermilk
2	eggs

Preheat oven to 475°.

Place butter in 10-inch skillet and place in pre-heated oven.

In large bowl, combine cornmeal, baking powder, baking soda and salt.
Mix well. In another bowl, beat eggs slightly, add buttermilk to eggs
and mix to combine. Add wet to dry ingredients and stir until
just combined.

Take skillet from oven and swirl butter in pan to coat. Pour remaining
butter into cornmeal mixture and stir, then pour into skillet.

Bake in 475° oven 25 minutes or until golden brown.

Serves 6-8

easy
can do ahead

Variations:

To make bread less hot, cut down on amount of peppers. For hot pepper lovers, fresh jalapeños work nicely in place of canned. Instead of canned corn, try fresh corn sautéed or boiled and cut from the cob. Also try adding 1-2 teaspoons fresh chopped cilantro.

Ike Hudson's Jalapeño Cornbread

This is a very hardy and spicy cornbread.

2½	cups corn meal
1	cup flour
2	tablespoons sugar
1	tablespoon salt
4	teaspoons baking soda (1 teaspoon if self rising cornmeal and flour are used)
4	eggs
1½	cups milk
½	cup cooking oil plus extra oil for pan
1	16-ounce can creamed yellow corn
2	cups grated onion
8	ounces minced or mashed jalapeño peppers
2	cups grated sharp cheddar cheese

Preheat oven to 400°.

Place heavily-greased 9x11-inch pan in oven while it heats.

Combine dry ingredients into bowl.

Beat eggs lightly, then add milk and oil to eggs. Pour into dry mixture. Add corn, peppers and onions and combine.

When oven reaches 400°, remove pan and fill with batter. Top batter with cheese. Bake about 30 minutes, until done.

Allow to cool 15-20 minutes before cutting.

Serves 6-8

easy
can do ahead

Cranberry Cornbread

*This cornbread is slightly nutty and fruity but not sweet. It is also won-
derful in cornbread dressing.*

1	cup whole kernel frozen corn
1	cup cranberries
¼	cup walnuts

1	cup cornmeal
1	cup flour
½	cup sugar
2½	teaspoons baking powder
¼	teaspoon salt

2	eggs, separated
1⅓	cups milk
½	cup melted butter

Preheat oven to 375°.

Grease large iron skillet with vegetable cooking spray and place in oven
while it preheats.

In medium-large bowl, mix together first 3 ingredients. In small bowl,
combine dry ingredients and add to corn mixture.

Lightly beat 2 egg yolks and combine with milk and butter. Add to
corn mixture. Beat two egg whites until stiff and fold into mixture.

Pour mixture into hot skillet and bake in 375° oven for about
45 minutes.

Serves 10-12

*can do ahead
can freeze*

Cook's Tip:

*If your cornbread
browns on top before
insides cook fully,
cover lightly with
aluminum foil to
finish baking for a
few extra minutes.*

Peggy's Special Hushpuppies

2½ cups self-rising corn meal mix
¼   cup flour
¼   cup sugar
3   tablespoons dill weed
1   teaspoon sage
2   eggs
1   medium onion, chopped
1½ cups buttermilk or beer
    oil for cooking

Mix all ingredients except oil. If too stiff, add a little water. If mixture is too soft and comes apart in frying, add a little meal. Heat oil in skillet. Drop batter by tablespoonful into hot oil. Hushpuppies will turn over by themselves. Cook until brown. Drain on paper towel and keep hot in warm oven until ready to serve with fish or seafood.

Serves 5 or 6

easy
can do ahead
can freeze

Puffy Popovers

1   tablespoon melted butter
2   large eggs, lightly beaten
¼   teaspoon salt or to taste
1   cup milk
1   cup all-purpose flour
1½ tablespoons cold butter

Cook's Tip:
Popovers can be filled when cold with sweet custard (page 200) as a dessert or chicken salad (page 68) for a luncheon.

Preheat oven to 450°.

In medium mixing bowl, combine melted butter, eggs, salt and milk. Add flour and beat with wooden spoon until mixture reaches consistency of heavy cream.

Cut cold butter into 6 pieces and put into 6 cups of ungreased muffin tin. Place muffin tin in warming oven just long enough to melt butter, then remove. Be careful not to burn butter.

Pour batter into muffin tin, filling cups ½-¾ full. Cook in 450° oven for 20 minutes, then reduce heat to 350° and continue baking 15-20 minutes until popovers are golden brown. Serve immediately.

Makes 6 popovers

 easy

Naan

This Indian yeast bread is particularly good for sopping up savory sauces in curries and stews.

2 cups warm water
1 teaspoon yeast
2 cups whole wheat flour
3 cups bread flour
2 teaspoons salt

In large bowl, combine warm water and yeast. Stir and allow yeast to dissolve, about 5 minutes.

Add whole wheat flour to water and yeast and stir about 1 minute in same direction to develop gluten. Scrape down sides with spatula and cover with plastic wrap. Let sit 1 hour.

Combine salt and 1 cup bread flour, add to dough and stir well. Continue adding flour and stirring until dough is too stiff to stir. Turn out onto well-floured surface and knead about 10 minutes or until dough is smooth and elastic. This should be a very soft dough.

Place dough in large, oiled bowl and turn over to coat with oil. Cover with plastic wrap and allow to double, 1-2 hours.

Punch down dough and divide into 4 pieces. Shape each piece into 7 to 8-inch circle. Cover with plastic wrap for about 20 minutes. Meanwhile, preheat oven to 450°. Place pizza stone, if you have one, on lowest rack of oven while preheating.

One at a time, shape breads into 12 to 14-inch circles by gently stretching dough. Using both hands, place bread on heated stone, or place bread circles on large, lightly oiled pizza pan and place in oven.

Bake 4-5 minutes or until brown on bottom. Serve with curries, stews, or any dish with lots of sauce.

Makes 4 flat breads

 *can do ahead*

Variation:
For a quick food processor version, dissolve yeast in water. Place both flours and salt in processor and combine. With machine running, pour yeast and water through food chute. Process until dough cleans sides of bowl. Turn off machine and let dough rest 10 minutes. Turn machine back on for 30-40 seconds. Remove dough to oiled bowl and let rise until doubled, 1-2 hours. Punch down and proceed with recipe.

Focaccia Bread

Whether soft or crisp, thin or thick, focaccia is typically flavored with herbs and olive oil.

2	packages dry yeast
½	cup warm water (110°)
8	cups bread or all-purpose flour, divided
2	tablespoons olive oil
2	teaspoons salt
2½	cups warm water (110°)
	olive oil
	kosher salt

Dissolve yeast in ½ cup warm water. Set aside until bubbly.

Mix 6½ cups flour, 2 tablespoons olive oil and salt. Add yeast mixture and remaining water.

Either by hand or machine, knead dough until smooth and elastic, adding additional flour as needed, to make a very soft dough. Place in large greased bowl, cover and store in warm place until doubled, about 1½ hours.

Preheat oven to 400°.

Punch down dough and cut into 2 pieces. Place each on its own large, well-greased baking sheet and flatten each to a 12-inch round ½-inch thick. Using thumb, make indentation in dough. Brush evenly with olive oil. Cover and let rise 30 minutes. Sprinkle with kosher salt. Bake at 400° until golden brown, 20-25 minutes.

Makes 2 12-inch loaves

easy
can do ahead
can freeze

"Focaccia derives its name from the Latin word focus, meaning 'hearth,' and evolved from the unleavened hearth cake eaten during the Middle Ages. It was made by patting the dough into a flat round and cooking it directly on a hot stone or under a mound of hot ashes. While it has become a popular national dish, its true home is the area around Genoa."

Angie Hamlet,
Woodward parent

Variations:

Add 3 tablespoons of fresh herbs (basil, sage or rosemary) and knead into dough, or sprinkle dough with dried basil, other herbs or chopped olives, along with kosher salt prior to baking.

Cheddar Cheese Biscuits

2	cups plain flour
3	teaspoons baking powder
1	tablespoon sugar
1	teaspoon salt
¼	teaspoon cayenne pepper
½	cup grated Parmesan cheese
4	tablespoons butter
4	tablespoons shortening
1½	cups grated cheddar cheese
¾	cup milk

Preheat oven to 450°.

Mix flour, baking powder, sugar, salt, cayenne, and Parmesan cheese in food processor. Cut in butter and shortening by pulsing until the consistency of coarse meal. Add cheddar and pulse 2 or 3 times until well distributed in flour mixture. Add milk and process only until soft dough forms.

Turn onto floured board and roll and pat until dough is about ½-inch thick. Cut with 2-inch biscuit cutter. Re-roll remaining dough, handling as little as possible. Cut remaining biscuits.

Place on ungreased cookie sheet and bake in 450° oven 12-13 minutes. Serve immediately or freeze. Reheat frozen biscuits for 5-7 minutes in 425° oven before serving.

Makes 20 biscuits

can do ahead
can freeze

"My grandmother makes me biscuits when I go home.

The aroma of the warm, soft bread seems to roam,

Floating from room to room until it reaches me.

Then I know in my heart it is supper time.

Spreading the butter on the bread comes easily,

All because my grandmother worked so hard,

just to make biscuits for me. "

Holly Wiggins,
seventh grade
Woodward student

Cook's Tip:

If not using food processor, cut butter, shortening, and cheese into flour with a pastry blender. Add milk and stir only until dough comes together.

Volunteers and Contributors

A world of well-deserved thank-yous to all of the Woodward family members who have participated in this Parents Club project. We gratefully acknowledge all of our volunteers who have generously shared their homes, recipes, time, artistic talents and ideas. You have made this Parents Club dream a reality. The recipes in this book have been triple-tested and fine-tuned to bring the world a cookbook as deliciously diverse as our own school. May this tempting collection of regional and international favorites happily challenge the boundaries and warm the hearth of every kitchen it reaches.

Marcia Abernethy	Pegi Black	Mary Ann Crossfield	Marie Gilbert
Kathy Accardi	Melanie Bodner	Rowena Davison	Lorraine Gilman
Wendy Acker	Sally Boice	Elizabeth Day	Pam Gilman
Debbie Aftuck	Joy Boone	Arline Deacon	Marixie Gilrane
Dennis Ainsworth	Hedy Borenstein	Tanya Deal	Cindy Goldberg
Marcy Allen	Judie Bowen	Vicky DeWulf	Cydney Goldberg
Teresa Allen	Suzanne Boyette	Elizabeth Dodson	Jane Goldner
Kathy Anderson	Patricia Brand	Linda Dorough	Roni Gossman
Lisa Anderson	Patti Bregman	Ann Douglas	Dorothy Green
Jeanine Andrews	Christi Brennan	Cheryl Dugal	Nancy Green
Cathalene Anegundi	Connie Brezina	Susan Dundee	David Greene
Lydia Appel	Connie Brinkley-Mebane	Ed Durden	Judith Greene
Pam Apple	Marilynn Broker	Jenny Durden	Sonya Gregory
Linya Araim	Barbara Brown	Mary Dykes	Jennifer Gresham
Mary Kay Armstrong	Dana Brown	Karima Eboo	Jeri Groves
Deborah Ashendorf	Linda Buchan	Sheila Edelson	Susan Guest
Bonnie Aspinwall	Dede Burnette	Mary Ellen Eley	Kiran Gupta
Elizabeth Avera	Moira Busby	Jacques Elfersy	Ellie Guthrie
Arlene Axelrod	Karen Buscovich	Beth Ellis	Carolyn Haldeman
Lynn Ayers	Sandra Butcher	Mary Elzy	Angie Hamlet
Barbara Babbit	Ann Butler	Patty Engstrom	Rachel Hammer
Joel Babbit	Cathy Butler	Sharon Eubanks	Keke Hammonds
Phyllis Baines	Margaret Camac	Diane Fanning	Jean Hanger
Delores Baker	Janet Camp	Martha Farrell	Avarita Hanson-Alexander
Joanne Baker	Constance Cantrell	Karen Farrugia	Lisa Hardin
Susan Baker	Cindy Cardin	Anne Faulkner	Joann Harris
Claudia Baldowski	Helen Carlock	Chris Fauls	Barbara Hart
Sandra Baldwin	Lori Carnes	Jenny Ferguson	Carol Hatfield
Nan Banks	Jill Carter	Mina Ferguson	Betty Hays
Eleanor Barnett	Shari Carter	Susan Fine	Isabell Hebberger
Gale Barnett	Sally Chafin	Diana Fister	Shelley Heckenberg
Wendy Barnhart	Jeanne Chambers	Carol Flannigan	Rosalie Heerdegen
Marcy Bass	Joann Chapman	Cindy Florence	Donna Heinzelmann
Martha Bass	Nancy Charles-Columbia	Linda Fontanelli	Jean Henard
Dorothy Bassett	Anna Cheak	Lynn Ford	Sue Henderson
Kimberly Battistini	Ivy Cheezem	Pat Ford	Betsy Hendrix
Barbara Baxt	Beverly Clemmer	Jan Fortune	Carol Henwood
Cheryl Baxter	Judi Clemmons	Lynda Fraizer	Erestene Herring
Anne Beerman	Sherrie Cleveland	Viki Freeman	Beth Hoats
Joel Beerman	Nancy Cole	Nancy Friedberg	Owen Hoffman
Debbie Bennett	Mary Collier	Jackie Fuller	Christine Holladay
Judi Benoff	Martha Conaway	Janet Funk	Patti Holman
Jan Benton	Cheryl Connell	Marcia Gaddis	Jane Holt
Cynthia Berger-Parent	Anne Constantine	Elyse Gainor	Joanne Hood
Lynn Berkowitz	Donna Corrales	Nancy Gallups	Rima Houssami
Carol Bernstein	Pat Corrales	Myrna Garron	Candi Howington
Burnie Berry, Jr.	Peggy Cosby	Patty Geltz	Kathryn Huddleston
Nancy Bivins	Shelby Crain	Charles Gibson	Ike Hudson
Faith Black	Pat Critelli	Vicki Gibson	Martha Hunt

Mary Ellen Hunter
Terri Hutchins
Barbara Hutto
Anne Jackson
Tom Jackson
Vicki Jackson
Vernyce Jenrette
Jeri Jesson
Janie Jeter
Margaret Johnson
Jan Johnston
Ala Jones
Judy Jones
Penny Jones
Maggui Joyner
Dawn Kane
Julie Keeter
Susan Kelley
Pat Kennedy
Natalie Kimball
Beth King
Carole Klug
Samantha Kluglein
Cecilia Koby
Ellen Koransky
Nancy Korzeniewski
Kathryn Krause
Leslie LaBriola
Sandra Lamb
Ann Lassiter
Claire Law
Chris Layfield
Darlene Lee
Dede Leff
Rich Leff
Corrine Leibrandt
Clara Lievano
Kathi Lemann
Dale Levenson
Jan Levine
Ruth Levison
Meryl Levitt
Lineve Lewis
Pat Lightner
Marian Lochry
Robbin Lorenzo
Deborah Low
Mary Jo Lund
Dawn Lundell
Carol Lunsford
Stella Lycouris
Kathy Madden
JoAnne Majeska
Precy Mallari
Christi Anna Mallia
Patty Mallicote
Faye Martin
Joanne Martin
Mickie Mathes
Robin Maxam

Nancy Maxwell
Betty Mays
Amy Mazzetta
Tito Mazzetta
Billie McCorkle
Henry McEnerny
Ruth McGehee
Barbara McGuire
Deborah McGuire
Cookie McKay
Doug McKay
Debbie McKelvey
Lou Jean McKnight
Peggy McNash
Barbara Mendel
Marie Menn
Susan Mercer
Sylvia Mercer
Kimberly Meredith
Curtis Miles
Elaine Miles
Ellen Milholland
Anne Miller
Lee Anne Mimbs
Donald Mitchell
Judy Mitchell
Tracy Monacell
Barbara Montaldi
Gay Moore
Dianne Morgan
Jaclynn Morris
Kathleen Morris
Patti Morrow
Kay Mortens
Chere Mortensen
Melonie Moseley
Jeanne Mull
Lynn Murphy
Presh Murray
Patty Nathan
Dana Naylor
Susan Neckman
Carol Nicholson
Jane Nicholson
Dee Nixon
Marilyn Noland
Allison Norfleet
Marie Nygren
Malissa O'Connor
Paul O'Connor
Gail Ohrstrom-Nguyen
Patty Olson
Kay O'Neal
Natalie Overman
Joe Palin
Mary Palin
Winnie Pannell
Linda Pappas
Laurie Parks
Cindy Peaden

Sandy Peaden
Trisha Pearson
Libba Pickett
Nancy Pinkerton
Elizabeth Plunkett-Buttimer
Margaret Porche
Mary Prebula
Marcia Price
Charlotte Pritchett
Carol Rainey
Deborah Reahm
Judy Reed
Nancy Reinhold
Jan Remington
Bunny Renkin
Candy Rhinehart
Patsy Rhodes-Rogers
Patty Richardson
Selma Ridgway
Diann Rifkin
Jean Rivas
Patti Robbins
Andrea Rohaly
Susan Rosenbleeth
Barbara Ross
Millie Ross
Deborah Rothman
Susan Rothman
Jean Rozema
Elizabeth Ruppersburg-King
Terri Saldona
Missy Sanchez
Franeen Sarif
Margo Savitz
Lorraine Sayer
Suzy Scheinberg
Robert Scherer
Amanda Scott
Janet Scott
Pam Server
Jane Shah
Meri Shakespeare
Loretta Shattles
Theda Shaw
Lisa Sherrill
Julie Shonkoff
Sylvia Shugart
Janet Simpson
Marion Simpson
Gay Singleton
Kathleen Skinner
Sandra Slider
Debbie Slimp
Becky Smith
Kathy Smith
Rhoda Sosebee
Lydia Sparger
Lynn Spurlin
Debbie Steele
Peggy Stevens

Marie Story
Sue Stovall
Nan Straughn
Jill Suchik
Terri Sunderland
Prue Sutton
Jade Sykes
Leandra Talentina
Heather Tangren
Kathy Tatum
Jan Taylor
Robin Taylor
Daniel Teahan
Barbara Teck
Cheryl Teets
Jean Temple
Sally Thomas
Jane Thrash
Debbie Torbush
Bonnie Townsend
Jeff Treadway
Lori Treadway
Barbara Trivedi
Deborah Troxell
May Tzou
Jane Van Epps
Amy Vassey
Rebecca Vaughn
Kari Velazco
Katie Velazco
Alec Velazco
Kathryn Voreis
Nancy Wagner
Donna Walker
Mary Ware
Catherine Waters
Margaret Watkins
Carol Weiss
Judy Weldon
Deborah Wells
Martha Wells
Fonde Werts
Ann Whatley
Missy White
Sharon White
Meg Whitlock
Beth Widener
Nita Willard
Cindy Williams
Roberta Williams
Teresa Williams
Terri Williams
Fonda Wilson
Valerie Wilson
Ed Wooller
Jan Young
Pat Young

INDEX

THE WORLD AT OUR TABLE
WOODWARD ACADEMY
1662 RUGBY AVENUE
COLLEGE PARK, GA 30337

Please send me _____ copies of **THE WORLD AT OUR TABLE** at $17.95 EACH, plus $3.50 handling and shipping. **(GEORGIA RESIDENTS ADD 6% SALES TAX.)** Payable in U.S. funds. **Make checks payable to The World At Our Table.**

Enclosed is my check or money order in the amount of $ _____

Please charge my: (circle one)   MC VISA

CARD # _____ EXP _____

SIGNATURE _____

NAME _____

_____

ADDRESS _____

_____

CITY _____

STATE _____ ZIP _____

DAYTIME PHONE (_____) _____

Prices are subject to change without notice.

THE WORLD AT OUR TABLE
WOODWARD ACADEMY
1662 RUGBY AVENUE
COLLEGE PARK, GA 30337

Please send me _____ copies of **THE WORLD AT OUR TABLE** at $17.95 EACH, plus $3.50 handling and shipping. **(GEORGIA RESIDENTS ADD 6% SALES TAX.)** Payable in U.S. funds. **Make checks payable to The World At Our Table.**

Enclosed is my check or money order in the amount of $ _____

Please charge my: (circle one)   MC VISA

CARD # _____ EXP _____

SIGNATURE _____

NAME _____

_____

ADDRESS _____

_____

CITY _____

STATE _____ ZIP _____

DAYTIME PHONE (_____) _____

Prices are subject to change without notice.

THE WORLD AT OUR TABLE
WOODWARD ACADEMY
1662 RUGBY AVENUE
COLLEGE PARK, GA 30337

Please send me _____ copies of **THE WORLD AT OUR TABLE** at $17.95 EACH, plus $3.50 handling and shipping. **(GEORGIA RESIDENTS ADD 6% SALES TAX.)** Payable in U.S. funds. **Make checks payable to The World At Our Table.**

Enclosed is my check or money order in the amount of $ _____

Please charge my: (circle one)   MC VISA

CARD # _____ EXP _____

SIGNATURE _____

NAME _____

_____

ADDRESS _____

_____

CITY _____

STATE _____ ZIP _____

DAYTIME PHONE (_____) _____

Prices are subject to change without notice.

I would like to see **THE WORLD AT OUR TABLE** in the following stores.

Name _____ Phone _____

Address _____

Name _____ Phone _____

Address _____

Name _____ Phone _____

Address _____

I would like to see **THE WORLD AT OUR TABLE** in the following stores.

Name _____ Phone _____

Address _____

Name _____ Phone _____

Address _____

Name _____ Phone _____

Address _____

I would like to see **THE WORLD AT OUR TABLE** in the following stores.

Name _____ Phone _____

Address _____

Name _____ Phone _____

Address _____

Name _____ Phone _____

Address _____